D1259470

discard

excess copies

A SHORT HISTORY OF THE ANCIENT NEAR EAST

Siegfried J. Schwantes

BAKER BOOK HOUSE
Grand Rapids, Michigan

ISBN: 0-8010-8026-6

Fifth printing, September 1979

PHOTOLITHOPRINTED BY CUSHING - MALLOY, INC.
ANN ARBOR, MICHIGAN, UNITED STATES OF AMERICA
1 9 7 9

TO MY WIFE

FOREWORD

This book aims at supplying the need for a short and yet substantial history of the Ancient Near East in the English language. Such need arises periodically because all such books become obsolete due to the rapid increase of available archaeological information casting light on the ancient past. Only specialists are able to keep up with the constant stream of monographs and articles appearing in scholarly journals which perfect and refine our understanding of the early civilizations of the Fertile Crescent.

Some excellent works are available in English dealing with specific chapters of that history, such as religion and magic, wisdom literature, art and sciences, chronology, or covering only a limited geographic area such as Egypt, Assyria, Phoenicia, etc. Other books are too general in scope, and the student is at loss to visualize the political history of the different Near Eastern civilizations, which after all must always remain as the frame of reference for any other approach. The present survey is avowedly centered around the political history, without neglecting other areas of human interest.

My debt to standard works in the whole field of the Near Eastern civilizations is immense, and no less sincerely appreciated because specific acknowledgement is not possible.

CONTENTS

EGYPT	SUMER	AKKAD	ASSYRIA	BABYLON
Pre-Historic	Jemdet Nasr Period			
The Old Kingdom				
c. 2850 B.C. Proto-Dynastic				
I Dynasty Menes				
II Dynasty	Early Dynastic			
c. 2650 The Pyramid Age				
III Dynasty Djoser				
IV Dynasty Kheops				
Khefren				
Mykerinos, etc.		**LAGASH**		
c. 2480 V Dynasty Sehure	I Dynasty of Ur	Ur-nansha		
Unas	Meshannipadda	Eannatum		
VI Dynasty Teti	Aannipadda			
Pepi II		Urukagina		
c. 2350	Lugalzaggisi of Uruk			
	THE AKKADIAN EMPIRE (2350-2150)			
	Sargon of Agade			
	GUTI INVASION			
VII and VIII Dynasties		**LAGASH**		
I Intermediate Period		Urbaba		
c. 2190-2052		Gudea		
	III Dyn. of Ur			
2052-2010 Mentuhotep II	Urnammu	**LARSA**		
2010-1998 Seankhare-Mentu hotep	Shulgi	Naplanum		
	Shusin			
XI Dynasty	Ibbisin			
	ISIN			
	Ishbi-irra			
XII Dynasty			Ilushuma	
1991-1972 Amenemhet I	Lipit-ishtar			
1971-1930 Sesostris I				I Dynasty
1929-1898 Amenemhet II				Sumuabum
1897-1879 Sesostris II				Sumulailu
1878-1841 Sesostris III			Irishum	
1840-1792 Amenemhet III			Sharrukin I	
II Intermediate Period		Waradsin	Shamsi-Adad I	Hammurabi
1778-c. 1570	Rimsin (1758-1698)	(1758-1698)	Ishme-Dagan I	(1728-1686)
XIII and XIV Dynasties				

EGYPT	ASSYRIA	BABYLON	HITTITES	MITANNI
c. 1670-1570 Period of the Hyksos XV and XVI Dynasties	Bel-bani			
c. 1610 XVII Dyn. Sekenenre Kamose	Li-tar-Sin	Ammizaduga	Labarna I	
1570 XVIII Dynasty				
1570-1545 Amosis	Irishum III		Hattusilis I	
1545-1524 Amenophis I	Shamshi-Adad II	Samsuditana	Mursilis I (Sack of Babylon)	
1524-c 1502 Thutmosis I, II	Ishme-Dagan II	KASSITE DYNASTY		
	Ashur-nirari I	Agum II		
1501-1480 Hatshepsut	Puzur-Ashur III	Barnaburiash I	Hantilis	
1502-1448 Thutmosis III		Kastiliash I	Telipinus	
1448-1422 Amenophis II		Ulamburiash		
1422-1413 Thutmosis IV				Shaushatar
1413-1377 Amenophis III	Ashur-nadin-ahhe	Kurigalzu I		Tushratta
1377-1358 Amenophis IV	Eriba-Adad I		Suppiluliumas	
1358-1349 Tutankhamun	Ashur-uballit I			Mattiwaza
1349-1345 Eye		Barnaburiash II		
XIX Dynasty	Arik-den-ilu			
1345-1318 Haremhab			Mursilis II	
Ramesses I	Adad-nirari I			
1317-1301 Seti I			Muwatalli	
1301-1234 Ramesses II	Shalmaneser I		Urhi-Teshup Hattusilis III	
1284-c. 1220 Merneptah	Tukulti-Ninurta I	Kastiliash IV		
Seti	Ashur-nadin-apli			
Siptah	Enlil-kudur-usur			
Irsu	Ninurta-apal-ekur		End of Hittite Empire	
1200 XX Dynasty		Enlil-nadin-ahhe		
1200-1197 Sethnakht		II DYNASTY OF ISIN		
1197-1165 Ramesses III	Ashur-dan I	Nebuchadnezzar I		
1165-1085 Ramesses IV-XI	Tiglathpileser I (c. 1116-1078)	(c. 1128- ?)		

	ASSYRIA	EGYPT	KINGDOM OF ISRAEL	BABYLON
c. 1116–1078	Tiglathpileser I	XXI Dynasty (1085–c. 950)	Period of the Judges	Nabu-mukin-apli
1049–1031	Ashurnasirpal I		Saul / David	
1010–970	Ashur-rabi II		Solomon	
969–965	Ashur-reshishi II	XXII Dynasty		
964–933	Tiglathpileser II	Shishak I		
932–910	Ashur-dan II			
909–891	Adad-nirari II			
890–884	Tukulti-Ninurta II			
883–859	Ashur-nasir-apli II	Osorkon II		
858–824	Shalmaneser III			Marduk-balatsu-iqbi
823–811	Shamsi-Adad V			
810–783	Adad-nirari III			
782–772	Shalmaneser IV			
771–754	Ashur-dan III	Shishak V		
753–744	Ashur-nirari V			
743–726	Tiglathpileser III			Pulu
725–721	Shalmaneser V			
721–705	Sargon II	XXIII, XXIV Dynasties / XXV Dynasty		Marduk-apal-iddina
704–681	Sennacherib	Shabako		Sennacherib
680–669	Esarhaddon	Shabitko		Asarhaddon
668–c. 630	Ashurbanipal	Taharqo / Tanutamun / Psammetichus I		Shamash-shum-ukin / Kandalanu
c. 630–628	Ashur-etil-ilani	Neco II (609–593)		Nabopolassar
c. 627–612	Sin-shar-ishkun			Nebuchadnezzar (604–562)
612–609	Ashur-uballit			Amel-Marduk / Nergal-shar-usur / Labashi-Marduk / Nabonidus
		Psammetichus II / Apries / Amasis		

KINGDOM OF ISRAEL (divided monarchy)

JUDAH: Rehoboam, Asa, Jehoshaphat, Jehoram, Ahaziah, Athaliah, Joash, Amaziah, Azariah, Jotham, Ahaz, Hezekiah, Manasseh, Amon, Josiah, Jehoahaz, Jehoiakim, Jehoiachin, Zedekiah (597–586)

ISRAEL: Jeroboam I, Baasha, Elah, Omri, Ahab, Ahaziah, Joram, Jehu, Jehoahaz, Jehoash, Jeroboam II, Zachariah, Menahem, Pekah, Hoshea (Fall of Samaria) 722/21

Note: Dates are given as a rule for kings in only one column to avoid overcrowding the chart. Kings on the same line are usually contemporaneous for at least part of their reign. The list of Kings in one column is representative but not necessarily complete.

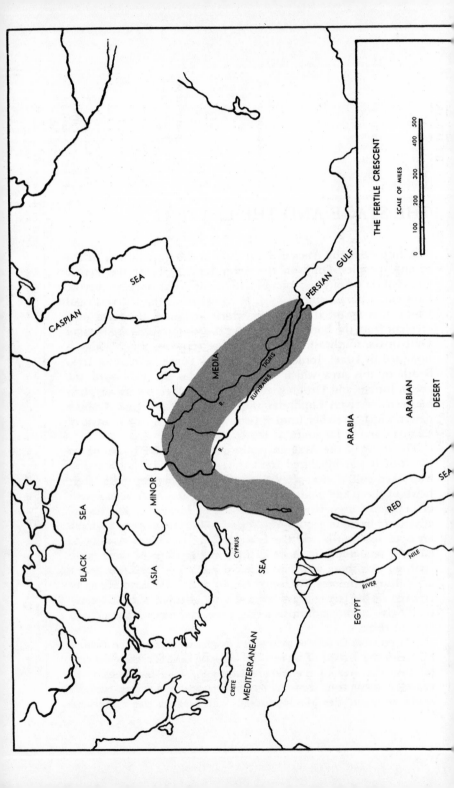

1

THE STAGE AND THE PLAYERS

A history of the Ancient Near East is chiefly a history of the Semitic peoples. Only on the outer boundaries of the Fertile Crescent do we meet peoples of a different racial stock. By Fertile Crescent, a phrase coined by J. H. Breasted of the University of Chicago, is meant the territory which arches in the form of a crescent from the border of Egypt in the southwest to the Persian Gulf in the southeast. It comprises the territory which today is occupied by Israel, Jordan, Syria, part of Turkey and all of Irak. South of this area which roughly includes the valleys of the rivers Jordan and Orontes, and the broad Mesopotamian plain between the rivers Euphrates and Tigris, lies the bleak Arabian desert which stretches from a point as far north as the oasis of Palmyra and as far south as the Indian Ocean.

The heart of the Arabian peninsula and of the Syrian desert north of it was inhabited from times immemorial by bedouins who eked out a near-starvation existence roaming with their herds of sheep and goats over the vast expanses of sand in search of better pastures. Under the pressure of hunger or the lust of adventure bedouin groups would raid from time to time adjacent areas of the "sown" on the fringe of the desert, eventually to adopt a semi-nomadic mode of life, in imitation of their more civilized neighbors who had already made the transition to an agricultural economy. Attracted by the more abundant life to be enjoyed in the fertile areas beyond their horizon, they did eventually give up nomadism to settle down and absorb the culture around them.

It is possible to follow with some degree of accuracy in historical times the arrival of wave after wave of nomads from the desert into the area of the Fertile Crescent. The first Semites to abandon nomadism seem to have been the Akkadians who already occupied the Mesopotamian valley when the Sumerians

settled on its southern border by the Persian Gulf. The Akkadians cross the limelight of history in the second half of the third
millenium B.C. when Sargon and his dynasty established a short-
lived empire, but their advent to Mesopotamia must antedate
this event by several centuries.

Next came the *Amurru* (Biblical Amorites) whom the Akkadians called "people from the west." There is evidence that the
Amurru pushed both to the east and to the west from the Syrian
desert. The zenith of their political power was attained with the
First Dynasty of Babylon in the days of Hammurabi. Contemporaneous with the migration of the Amorites must have been the
penetration of the Canaanites into the territory which came to
be known as Palestine. A branch of the Canaanites pushed
farther to the northwest towards the Mediterranean coast and
appear in history as the Phoenicians.

Late in the second millennium the Arameans begin to give up
their nomadic habits, and by and by occupy the region around
Damascus in Syria, while at the same time pouring into the territory by the river Khabur in Upper Mesopotamia where they
established several principalities collectively known as *Aram
Naharaim*. Somewhat later is the arrival of the Chaldeans, closely
related to the Arameans, who settle in the lower portion of the
Mesopotamian valley. Foiled several times in their attempt to
control Babylon, they finally succeeded in the late seventh century, inaugurating the brilliant, though short-lived, Neo-Babylonian Empire.

Still later is the infiltration of the Nabateans who settled in
the southern and eastern edges of Palestine building up a prosperous kingdom just prior to the Christian era. Last but not
least was the eruption of the Arabian tribes into the territory of
the Byzantine empire in the seventh century of our era under
the impetus of a great religious enthusiasm which carried their
victorious hosts as far as Spain in the west and India in the east.

The sound of the clash between the roving bedouins and the
settled populations on the fringe of the desert is clearly perceived
in the earliest documents of Mari, Babylon, and in the pages of
the Old Testament. We read of the raid of Midianite tribes
across the Jordan in the period of the Judges, for example. The
restless bedouin gradually settles down, adopts an agrarian mode
of life, absorbs a modicum of civilization, and finally makes himself master of the territories his ancestors coveted.

Common to all peoples mentioned above is their language
which scholars call Semitic. There are clear affinities between all

Semitic dialects pointing to a single original linguistic stock. Through a scientific study of these affinities linguists try to recover Protosemitic, the ideal parent language which gave rise to all known variants in Akkadian, Arabic, Hebrew, Phoenician, etc. In this search Semiticists are much better situated than their confrères in the field of Indo-European languages since they have a much older and richer collection of documents with which to work.

In contrast with most European languages, Semitic languages have a typical guttural pronunciation, since beside the palatal consonants they have several pharyngeal and laryngeal articulations. Peculiar to all Semitic languages is also the fact that the majority of verbal roots consist of three consonants. The basic meaning of the root is determined by the consonants; the vowels as well as consonantal repetitions serve to modify the meaning of the root by the formation of different nominal and verbal stems and their inflections. This is particularly true in the domain of verbs and nouns derived from verbs. Originally vowels were not expressed in writing. They were supplied by the reader according to the context. Akkadian formed an exception to this rule since from the earliest times its writing was syllabic. This makes Akkadian especially useful in the study of Semitic phonology. In the case of the other languages vowels were introduced in the writing of religious texts when these languages ceased to be spoken in order to insure correct pronunciation. Such was the case of the Hebrew Bible and the Arabic Koran.

Akkadian originally had a very simple vowel system consisting of the three pure sounds a, i, u. This was also true in classical Arabic. Both languages also show a declension system of nouns, pronouns and adjectives. The singular of nouns had a nominative in -u, a genitive in -i, and an accusative in -a; the plural had a nominative in -ū, and an oblique case in -ī. Gradually all Semitic languages dropped case endings which were clearly observed as late as the Code of Hammurabi (c. 1700 B.C.).

Characteristic of Semitic languages is also the dual number and the fact that the second person of pronouns and verbs had two genders. As a rule they do not have the possessive pronouns of adjectival character, resorting to a pronominal suffix to express possession. Thus ben is "son," and beni is "my son" in Hebrew. Semitic languages are poor in descriptive adjectives. To qualify the material of which an object is made they resort to the use of a descriptive noun in apposition or in the genitive case. Thus in Arabic to translate "the silky dress" one would say *at-tubu l-harisu* "the dress the silk."

The verbal system of the Semitic languages is quite different from that of Indo-European languages. Properly speaking it has no "tense" such as past, present and future. It denotes only what is called "aspect," that is, it distinguishes state from action, and completed from incomplete action. The tense must be inferred from the context. The ambiguities are, nevertheless, much fewer than might be surmised. Semitic verbs are usually quoted in dictionaries and grammars not in the infinitive, but in the third person singular masculine of the perfect "tense," which is the simplest form of the verb. The Hebrew calls it the *Qal* form, that is, the light form because it is the least inflected.

In the matter of sentence construction Semitic languages make a typical distinction between "verbal" and "nominal" propositions. In verbal propositions the verb is stated first followed by its subject. Thus the normal order in the verbal proposition would be, "Wrote Isaiah..." and not "Isaiah wrote.." Nominal sentences have no verb, not even the copula "is" which must be understood. Thus in Hebrew one would simply say "Yahweh God" for "Yahweh is God." Subordination of sentences, as a rule, is not expressed and must be deduced from the context. Sentences are simply juxtaposed, and it is up to the reader in many cases to infer their relationship as relative, final, causal, etc.

The Semites not only spoke closely related dialects all derived from a common parent language, but also give evidence of many cultural and religious affinities which lead us to believe that they originally formed one racial group, just as the Indo-Aryan peoples are believed to be descendants of one common stock. We have mentioned the Semitic peoples of the Fertile Crescent and the chief characteristics of their language. A word should be said about the other peoples who also played a part in the drama of the Ancient Near East.

On the southeast border of Mesopotamia lived the Sumerians the creators of the earliest known civilization. Unhappily nothing is known for certain about the racial and linguistic affinities of this gifted people, even though the abundant literature they left hold today few mysteries to specialists. Being the vehicle of a higher culture, Sumerian contributed not a few words to the Akkadian vocabulary and through it to that of other Semitic languages.

East of Mesopotamia on the slopes of the Iranian Plateau lived, since the earliest times, the Elamites who borrowed most of their culture from their neighbors to the west. Their racial affinities remain obscure. About the first half of the second millennium the Iranian Plateau began to be overrun by Aryan peoples who appear to have migrated from some center in eastern Europe and crossed the Caucasus in successive waves. One of the earliest of these would be represented by the Hittites who turned westward after reaching Armenia and built an imposing civilization in Asia Minor. Another and perhaps more numerous branch turned eastward and migrated all the way to India where they brought about the collapse of the old Indus civilization. Stragglers of this Aryan movement settled in the territory of modern Iran, and after some centuries of quiet development burst into history as the Medes and Persians. Conquering Babylon in 539 B.C. they put an end to the Semitic dominance in the Levant for over a thousand years, and deserve therefore a special chapter in any history of the ancient Near East.

Outside the Fertile Crescent but not entirely immune to Semitic influences lay Egypt on the banks of the Nile. Its racial stock seems to be the result of a fusion of aboriginal peoples called Nilotic, and which may have migrated from the south into the Nile valley, with Hamitic tribes coming from the Arabian Peninsula. Thus the Egyptian language as known from the earliest inscriptions shows an older native strand on which a Semitic dialect exerted marked influence. A sprinkling of Semitic words is clearly recognizable together with many grammatical features obviously Semitic. Just to mention one example, the Egyptian pronoun of the first person singular was pronounced somewhat like *inek,* while the Akkadian was *anaku.*

Much has been said about the splendid isolation of Egypt which allowed its people several millennia of imperturbed development. In reality, though, Egypt never cared for absolute isolation, and this for simple commercial reasons. As early as the First Dynasty Egypt was importing cedar wood from Byblos in Phoenicia, and Egyptian grain and papyrus were in demand in Phoenicia and elsewhere. Ideas have a way of diffusing abroad through the avenues of trade, and there are reasons to believe that the art of writing was borrowed by Egypt from Mesopotamia, even though in the Nile Valley it followed its own distinctive line of development blossoming into the beautiful hieroglyphic writing.

Having briefly surveyed the land and the peoples who played a major role in the drama of the ancient Near East, we shall now focus our attention on the origins and growth of civilization in the valley of Mesopotamia.

2

EARLY MESOPOTAMIA

Archeological findings seem to indicate that culture spread from the mountains to the north of Mesopotamia gradually down the rivers Euphrates and Tigris towards the Persian Gulf. A typical site of neolithic culture is *Qala't Jarmo,* where only stone artifacts were found but no pottery. In the same stratum crude clay statuettes were discovered representing the animals which had been domesticated, e.g., the goat, the sheep, the dog, and the pig. There is evidence of cereals being ground between stones, but none that they were cultivated.

An advance in culture is found in *Tell Hassuna,* a pre-historic site twenty-five miles south of Mosul near ancient Nineveh. Here tools and weapons of flint and obsidian were discovered, as well as coarse pottery. Some cereals begin to be cultivated. Flint-toothed sickles were found, an evidence that reaping of cereals was practiced. Somewhat later adobe homes were built, and pottery improves in quality showing first decorations. Beads and amulets reveal an interest in personal adornment; figurines of the mother-goddess made of clay suggest the religious and magical ideas of the time.

The next cultural period is known as *Tell Halaf,* from its typical site on the Khabur river. Other sites where a similar level of culture was identified are Samarra, Tepe Sialk, and Tepe Gawra, where excavations were carried on by E. A. Speiser of the University of Pennsylvania. This culture represents a clear transition from nomadic to sedentary life. The first villages appear. The use of copper utensils, though rare, marks also the transition from the Neolithic to the Chalcolithic period. The most distinctive product of this culture is its excellent pottery. Even though hand-made, it ranks very high in quality. Vase painters make use of polychrome geometrical and floral designs to decorate the inside of shallow bowls and plat-

Covered wagon and dog excavated at Tepe Gawra.
Courtesy, University Museum, Philadelphia

Stela from Tell Halaf showing a wheeled chariot.
Courtesy, Aleppo Museum

The acropolis at Tepe Gawra.
Courtesy University Museum, Philadelphia

ters. Many samples have a genuine glaze paint, and pottery was fired at intense heat in closed kilns. From the painting on one vessel it is deduced that wheeled vehicles may have been invented at that time. There is also evidence that the arts of weaving and spinning were known to people of the Halafic culture.

Findings in Tepe Gawra in Assyria show a new technological advance — the discovery of the potter's wheel moved by hand. But this advance seems to have made pottery so commonplace, that it ceased to be a means to express higher spiritual needs. For a better guide to the spiritual ideals of the time we must look from now on to the architecture of temples and the fine engravings on stamp-seals. Smelting of copper replaces hammering in the manufacture of copper objects. Noticeable also is the use of regular bricks instead of clay for the erection of walls.

Al-'Ubaid Period

By this time culture had already spread to southern Mesopotamia, which soon takes the lead under the spur of a fertile but swampy soil which required drainage and irrigation for maximum productivity. Characteristic sites for this period are Al-'Ubaid, Susa, Ur, Warka, Eridu, etc.

Characteristic pottery found at Tell Al-'Ubaid is a fine, pale greenish ware, painted with free geometrical designs in black or dark brown. As already mentioned, the quality of the pottery declines as it becomes more popular. Excavations in Eridu, in the extreme south of Mesopotamia show how reed and mud houses give place to others made of brick. A very small temple of about 4x4 yards is replaced in the same site by larger ones, which finally attain the traditional form they would retain for many centuries. In Eridu, level VII, came to light a high temple built on a terrace. It is rectangular in form with groups of rooms on both sides of a larger middle room. In this are to be found a podium and an altar. The entrance is in one of the long sides. In the corresponding level in Tepe Gawra an acropolis was found with three large temples, one brown, one red, and one white, enclosing three sides of an open court. All showed recessed niches inside and outside apparently for strengthening the walls, as well as for decorative purposes.

By this time agriculture was widely practiced. Wheat, barley, millet, and other cereals were cultivated, and so were fruits

such as dates, olives, figs and grapes. Many sickles of clay or
flint have been found. Very likely they were set in a wooden
handle. The Euphrates overflows every year requiring the building of dikes, drainage of swamps by the river side, and the digging of irrigation ditches to extend the cultivable land. All of
this demanded a definite communal organization. Besides this,
dikes broke down, canals filled up with silt in a short time, so
that the whole irrigation system had to be kept up constantly.
This again made co-ordinated and persistent effort imperative.
The successful response of the population to the challenge presented by the environment brought about the Mesopotamian
civilization.

Graves for the dead are not dug at random, but located in
cemeteries. In Eridu one cemetery was excavated with one
thousand graves. Corpses lay either flat on their backs, or on
their side in a squatting position. Wares for food buried with
the dead were found, showing some belief in life beyond the
grave.

Whether villages were already united into larger political
units it is hard to say for this period. But the similarity of
culture over large areas favors the idea that a loose political
interdependence already existed. So we may speak of a Tepe
Gawra circle in the north, and of an Al-'Ubaid circle in the
south.

Uruk Period (c. 3500-3000 B.C.)

Typical sites for this period are Uruk or Warka (Biblical
Erech) Susa, Ur and Tepe Gawra. The culture of this period
shows a clear break with that of the preceding period. This
might suggest the occupation of Lower Mesopotamia by the
Sumerians. Their racial type and place of origin are still a
matter of debate. The Sumerian language, of agglutinative
type, is unaffiliated with any other known language. E-GAL and
LU-GAL illustrate what is meant by agglutinative. Words are
simply juxtaposed. Thus the first meant literally "big house"
and then by extension "palace" or "temple." It was adopted
by the Akkadian language, and from this passed into Hebrew
as hêkal "temple." LU-GAL is literally "big man," and then
by extension "king." What is certain is that the Sumerians,
whatever their place of origin, brought into Mesopotamia a
more advanced culture which influenced for all time the civilization of the Near East.

The pottery of this period shows little artistic skill, even though the firing technique is very good. Temple vessels are made of stone or metal. Excavations carried on by the Germans in the 1930's in Uruk show many occupational levels closely superimposed. The pattern of temples is a development of the previous period, with side rooms flanking an inner court. There were originally two temple sites in Uruk, one dedicated to the celestial god Anu, the other, to Inanna (Innin, identified by the Akkadians with Ishtar), the mother-goddess. The temple of Anu was built on an artificial terrace made of bricks, being a prototype of the later ziggurat, which became characteristic of the religious architecture of Mesopotamia. A seeming innovation is the revetment of the Uruk temples. The walls made of sun-dried bricks are covered with a thick layer of clay, which in turn is adorned with hundreds of cones of fired clay, the heads of which are colored either black, red or white. These clay cones were distributed in geometrical patterns, imitating the surface of a reed-mat.

An important invention of this period is that of writing. It originated with the need of recording economic transactions connected with the temples. At first writing was pictographic. Numerals were circular or half-circular marks on the clay tablets. Both the decimal and sexagesimal numerical systems were used. Later pictographic writing gave place to ideographic, and this in turn to syllabic. Among the primitive tablets found some are particularly interesting because they contain lists of signs, probably as a teaching device. This tradition of writing list of signs and dictionaries continued up to the beginning of our era, and has been a godsend to scholars. Since the oldest tablets were written in Sumerian, the Sumerians are credited with the invention of writing.

Preliminary work on the decipherment of cuneiform writing was done by G. F. Grotenfend. With the discovery and copy of the Behistun inscription by G. Rawlinson in 1847, containing a proclamation of Darius I of Persia in Babylonian, Elamite and old Persian, further progress in decipherment was made much more secure. The first to yield its secret to Rawlinson was old Persian written with relatively few cuneiform characters. This in turn became the clue to decipher the other two languages. Babylonian proved to be a Semitic language, showing therefore many affinities with Arabic and Hebrew, and before long specialists were translating the thousands of tablets which have come to light since. The existence of the Sumerian language soon became evident to scholars, first of all in religious texts, but it also has been gradually mastered by scholars.

From this period, too, dates the invention of the cylinder seal, which together with the ziggurat and the cuneiform writing characterize through the centuries the culture which blossomed in the valley between the Euphrates and the Tigris. The finely engraved cylinder seals became one of the most popular means for the expression of artistic and religious ideas. Utensils of gold and later of silver make their appearance marking another advance in culture.

The village eventually gives place to the temple-city. The state is organized under the assumption that everything, land, people, animals and plants, is the property of the deity. His representative is the *Lugal,* the "great man." His abode is the temple, in the stores of which the produce of the land and of the work of men is kept. The *Lugal* gives to each one his work and his reward. The artisans, priests, scribes, and soldiers settle around the temple forming the city proper. Sumerian society is a typical theocratic society.

Jemdet Nasr Period

The culture of this period which flourished in the first quarter of the third millennium B.C. left its impress upon all the Near-East: Elam, Iran, Asia Minor, Syria and probably Egypt (Negade II). The re-introduction of the stamp-seal, and of painted pottery seems to indicate some influence from Iran. In Uruk the temple of Innin is built on a terrace, and the worship of the mothergoddess seems to have replaced that of the sky-god Anu. Her worship is the main theme of engravings and sculptures of all sorts. Innin begins to appear in close association with the legendary king of Uruk, the semi-god Dumuzi whose Biblical equivalent is Tammuz (Ezekiel 8:14). He is represented in Sumerian poems both as shepherd and fisherman. Gradually the Innin-Dumuzi vegetation myth is evolved to reappear under different guises in many parts of the Near-East. So we shall find in Ugarit the myth of Baal and Anath, and later that of Adonis and Aphrodite in the Greek speaking areas of the Levant.

Metal is employed more freely, and the first use of bronze points to the dawning of the Bronze Age in Mesopotamia. Writing progresses in this period from the pure pictographic to the semi-pictographic stage. A tendency is noticeable to cut down the number of signs employed.

Early Dynastic Period

With this period, also known to historians as the Mesilim period, we cross the threshold of the historic period proper, since tablets from this time may be read with a fair degree of accuracy. The most important group of documents comes from Farah (Shuruppak). Some long texts illustrate how the script passed from the semi-pictographic stage to the syllabic. The use of wedges is introduced. By and by writing is used for purposes other than to record commercial transactions: edicts, religious compositions, inscriptions on votive objects, etc. The very progress towards syllabic writing reflects the prevailing tendency in this period to abstract thought.

Arts and crafts, as attested by the discoveries in the Royal cemeteries of Ur made by Sir Leonard Woolley, attain a very high level of perfection. Towns increase in size and begin to be fortified with walls. Uruk, for example, boasted of a wall six miles long with nine hundred towers. The Gilgamesh Epic ascribes this wall to the legendary Gilgamesh himself. Such fortifications suggest the unsettled conditions of the times.

Many archeological evidences point to a break between the culture of the Jemdet Nasr period and that of the Early Dynastic. Some of these are: First, a shift of the center of gravity of culture from the extreme south near the Persian Gulf to the north, in the neighborhood of modern Bagdad. Here we find Kish, the capital of king Mesilim, the first royal name on the king lists to be identified on a contemporary document. Second, the introduction of the plano-convex brick which seems a backward step. Third, the introduction of the custom of building temples on an excavated area filled with pure sand, as if to isolate the temples from the contaminating soil. This cultural break with the past may be explained by a strong influence of Semitic ideas radiating from Kish. Besides this, excavations in Uruk evince a shift in the social structure for no longer is the temple the center of city-life all by itself. The king begins to share the limelight together with the high-priest. The royal palace stands out as equally important in the evolving political order.

Several king lists are known from Mesopotamia, some of which try to bridge the obscure, prehistoric times with legendary dynasties. One of these is the Sumerian king list composed in the Isin-Larsa period, c. 1900 B.C. It begins with eight kings who ruled 241,000 years before the Flood. This is followed

The temple tower at Ur of the Chaldees in its present condition.
Courtesy, S. H. Horn

by a succession of dynasties: First, that of Kish credited with over 24,510 years; second, Uruk — twelve kings ruling 2,310 years; Third, Ur — four rulers for 177 years, and so down to the Isin-Larsa period. Beginning with the First dynasty of Ur it becomes a reliable historical record. The impression the list was intended to convey is that there was only one dynasty ruling at a time. But this is obviously incorrect. The document apparently was written to justify the right of Isin to be sole ruler in Sumer.

Time of the First Dynasty of Ur (c. 2500 B.C.)

The Sumerian king list mentions as first ruler of this dynasty *Meshannipadda,* supposed to have ruled eighty years. Excavations in Ur have brought to light his name, as well as that of his wife Nintur, and of his son Aannipadda, who built a temple in Al-'Ubaid in the vicinity of Ur to the goddess Ninhursag. Strangely the name of Aannipadda does not appear on the kings' list.

Many cities are known to have flourished in this period, and in some cases we are informed of the names of their kings and officers. Such were Mari, Ashur, Nippur, Shuruppak, Eridu, etc. But Ur seems to have enjoyed the political leadership. Of the splendor of its rulers testify the royal tombs famous for the exquisite gold ornaments of Queen Shubad, and the mass burial of servants to accompany their sovereigns to the other world. There is no evidence that these officials and dames were executed *en masse.* It is more likely that they willingly drank a cup of poison.

We are particularly well informed concerning the political history of Lagash, a rather small city, but whose remains were exceptionally well-preserved until brought to light in the third quarter of the last century by E. de Sarzec. Tablets from this site record the founding of a dynasty by *Ur-Nansha,* who used the title of *lugal.* His grandson *Eannatum* was an energetic ruler who campaigned against Elam and the neighboring city of Umma. To commemorate his triumph over Umma he erected the so-called Vulture Stela, found in 1878. It is covered on all sides with inscriptions and pictures in vertical columns. It is the best source of our knowledge of early Sumerian art, language, history and religio-political world-view. Eannatum appears on a war chariot at the head of his warriors, who are armed with lance and axe. Their own dead are depicted as receiving an honorable burial, while the dead of the enemy are given as prey to the vultures.

After three weak rulers the kingship passed to the hands of priests, who apparently were very unscrupulous. The people revolted and placed on the throne *Urukagina.* In the sixth year of his reign he introduced some important social reforms with the intent of making the lot of the poor more bearable, and restraining the greed of the priesthood. He has been deservedly called the first reformer in history.

But in the city of Umma *Lugalzaggisi* grows in power and conceives the idea of uniting all the city-states of Sumer under one ruler. In total disregard to precedent he attacks and destroys Lagash, subdues several other cities, and makes Uruk the capital of his kingdom. But his proud achievement, considered unpardonable *hybris* by his contemporaries, was short-lived. The Semite Sargon was soon to assert his power over all of Mesopotamia.

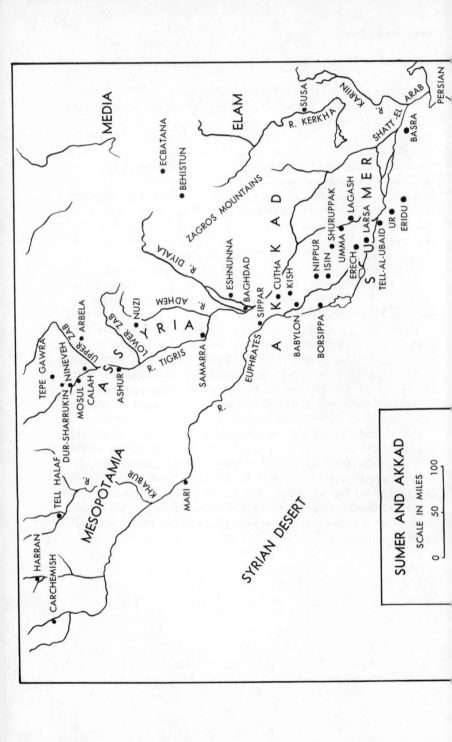

SUMER AND AKKAD

SCALE IN MILES

0   50   100

3

THE AKKADIAN EMPIRE

I. The Akkadian Empire (*c.* 2350-2150 B.C.)

The Semites who had been settling in Mesopootamia for several centuries, and who had by now thoroughly assimilated Sumerian culture, are ready to assume the political leadership of Mesopotamia. The founder of the Akkadian empire is *Sargon I*, whose military prowess made him a legendary figure in the Near East. From the position of butler of king Ur-Zababa of Kish he rises to the kingship. Through the use of better weapons and tactics he defeats Lugalzaggisi who was captured and made a prisoner in the temple of Enlil in Nippur. Sargon arming his troops with bow and spear and allowing them greater freedom of movement conquers Uruk, Ur, and finally all of Sumer to the Persian Gulf. Next he conquers Elam to the east, Subartu to the north, and Syria to the west from where the precious cedar was brought. He may even have crossed the Taurus Mountains, the so-called Silver Mountains, into Asia Minor. Some historians go so far as to credit him with the annexation of Greece, Crete and Cyprus to his territories. A tablet from his time representing the first attempt to draw a *mappa mundi* shows how much the conquests of Sargon were an object of admiration.

Sargon built a new capital, Agade, the exact location of which is today unkown. He surrounded himself with a splendid court, and boasted that fifty-four hundred people ate before him every day. More than half a century was spent by this giant in the erection of his empire.

His son *Rimus* had to subdue revolts in several parts of the realm, and in his ninth year fell victim to an assassin. His place was taken by his brother *Manistusu* who kept the empire together for another fifteen years. The grandson of Sargon,

Naramsin, again had to cope with widespread revolts; he defeated a coalition of thirty-two kings in Elam, and seized silver

Victory stela portraying
Naramsin with horns.
Courtesy, the Louvre

mines in Iran. His victory over the Lulabeans on the Iranian border is commemorated on a famous stela, which was later carried as a war trophy by the Elamites from the city of Sippar to Susa. On this stela Naramsin is portrayed with horns like a god. His greatest glory was the conquest of the land of Magan identified by some historians with Egypt, but more likely some territory in the south-east of the Arabian Peninsula.

In less than two centuries Akkadian culture spread all over

the Fertile Crescent. Sumerian language, culture and military art were superseded by that of the Akkadians. The state socialism of the Sumerian cities gave place to a centralized government, operated by a bureaucracy under the surveillance of the crown. Trade caravans follow everywhere in the wake of the army. The tension between the classes is forgotten in the splendor of world dominion.

The political ascendancy of Akkad is accompanied by the rising prestige of the Akkadian god Shamash, the sun-god of Sippar, son of the moon-god Sin. Together Shamash, Sin, and the Venus-goddess Ishtar Anunitu build the core of an Akkadian religion of astral character which contrasts with the agrarian religion of the Sumerians. But gradually there is an amalgamation of religious beliefs so that the Akkadian Sin comes to be identified with Nanna, and Ishtar with the mother-goddess Innin. Likewise there is a tendency to identify the sun-god Shamash with the vegetation-god Dumuzi of Ur.

The Akkadian Empire was the creation of one family of exceptionally able rulers. When its strength was exhausted the empire collapsed. The Gutians, semi-barbarians from the Zagros Mountains, took the opportunity to overrun Mesopotamia, which now languished during one century (2150-2050 B.C.) under their harsh rule. This is a period of cultural stagnation, and archeological finds have not illuminated the age to any great extent. Apparently of all Mesopotamia the land of Sumer suffered the least from the barbarian invasion, and the Sumerians were the first to rise against foreign domination.

II. Ur III Period (c. 2050-1950 B.C.)

The expulsion of the Gutians was achieved by *Utuhegal* of Uruk (Erech). But Utuhegal did not enjoy his victory long. His vassal, *Urnammu* of Ur, revolts against him and makes himself "king of Sumer and Akkad." He thus inaugurates the Third Dynasty of Ur which is able to hold the rule for about a century. Urnammu contents himself with ruling a kingdom that besides Sumer and Akkad included only North Mesopotamia and parts of Elam. His policy is not of conquest, but of building. He left a law-code found in Nippur many years ago, but only recently identified as such. Government appears strongly centralized with a very efficient bureaucracy.

Excavations in Ur brought to light a tablet in which Nabonidus, king of Babylon late in the seventh century B.C., and an amateur archeologist himself, refers to the discovery of an in-

scription of Urnammu and his son Shulgi, from which he concluded that the ziggurat which Urnammu had begun to build
was finished by his son. Nabonidus then adds that he repaired
the ziggurat with mortar and burned brick. Interestingly enough
a stela of Urnammu himself was discovered, in which the king
appears before the god Nanna, receiving the command to build
him a house. Thus the great temple tower of Ur came to be
built housing in its core the more modest constructions of previous generations. From a study of the ruins of Ur, Henry Frankfort concluded that the city had a population of about twenty-
four thousand people settled in an area of 150 acres.

Shulgi followed his father on the throne, but in his rule of
about fifty years did little to extend the borders of the kingdom. Like his father he was more interested in the building of
temples. Nippur appears as the most sacred city during this
dynasty. Tablets make clear that the country was divided into
districts to provide offerings each month for the shrines of
Nippur. Trade prospered in a climate of relative peace. One
important depot was on the island of Dilmun probably to be
identified with the island of Bahrein in the Persian Gulf. Another center of trade was in Cappadocia in Asia Minor, where
thousands of tablets have been found. Caravans of donkeys used
to ply the route between Assyria and Anatolia. Of one caravan
it is known that it transported twenty-seven thousand pounds of
merchandise on two hundred asses.

Shulgi was succeeded by *Amarsin, Shusin* and *Ibbisin,* whose
names indicate the popularity of the cult of the god Sin in
this period. The last named king was carried prisoner to Elam,
while the city of Ur was completely destroyed. A later poet wrote
in lamentation:

O my city attacked and destroyed, my city attacked without cause.
Behold the storm ordered in hate — the violence has not abated;
O my house of Sin in Ur, bitter is thy destruction.[1]

With the fall of Ur ends the last attempt of the Sumerians to
carry the leadership in Mesopotamia. But Sumerian religion
and culture continued to influence the Near East for many centuries longer. This enduring influence owes much to a genuine
revival of Sumerian culture at the end of the third millennium
as witnessed by the numerous literary documents of this age,
as well as by architectural monuments due to royal undertakings
in Ur and elsewhere.

1. James B. Pritchard, *Ancient Near Eastern Texts,* p. 461.

Not.least in revealing this last bloom of the Sumerian genius are the findings in Lagash. While the Third Dynasty was ruling in Ur, Gudea was an *ensi,* that is, a vassal king, in Lagash. He left so many sculptures of himself, and so many inscriptions, that no other Sumerian character is so well known as he. He

Gudea of Lagash in standing position.

Courtesy, the Louvre

built anew or renovated innumerable temples, in the foundations of which many barrel-shaped stones covered with inscriptions were found. These represent the oldest and most comprehensive texts in the Sumerian language, which have not only a historical but also a literary value. From all this Gudea shines forth as a very pious ruler, always busy in building temples, ever anxious for eternal life.

From Sumerian religious texts found in Nippur and elsewhere, there is evidence of a growing syncretism in religion, since a series of divine names appear as mere liturgical appelations of a single deity. Liturgies also indicate that worshipers tended to venerate a single god with whom they identified all other gods of the same class. The same tendency is traceable when the Babylonians identify Enlil with their god Marduk, while the Assyrians do the same with their national deity Ashur. But one cannot speak of strict henotheism in Babylon since Enlil, the storm-god of Nippur, is unquestioningly believed to rule the whole world.

4

THE AMORITES AS RULERS
OF MESOPOTAMIA

When Ibbisin, the last king of Ur, fell into the hands of
the Elamites, the unity of the kingdom of Sumer and Akkad
came to an end. Everywhere reappeared the old city states, no
longer under the leadership of native rulers, but of Elamites,
and, to a much greater extent, of Amorites. The Amorites
represent a new wave of Semites migrating from the western
desert into Mesopotamia. They show greater linguistic affinities
with the Canaanites of Syria and Palestine than with the Akkadians. As jumping boards for further expansion the Elamites
seize Larsa in the south, and the Amorites entrench themselves
in Mari in the Upper Euphrates.

From Mari comes the Amorite *Ishbi-irra* who succeeds in
carving for himself a principality in Isin, from where he subdued southern Mesopotamia as far as Ur. Another rival was the
Amorite *Naplanum* who was able to hold Larsa. Nevertheless
Isin under Ishbi-irra and his successors exerts the hegemony in
the land as if there were yet a kingdom of Sumer and Akkad.
The last of his line was *Lipit-ishtar,* justly famous for his law-
code, who was expelled to give place to another dynasty.

While Isin and Larsa carry on their rivalry, the Elamite
Kudur-Mabug carves for himself a principality in the mountains
of West Iran, Yamutbal. In Babylon the Amorite, *Sumu-abum,*
in turn makes himself an independent ruler. Greater than he
was his son *Sumulailu* who ruled thirty-six years, and encouraged the codification of law. Assyria, too, takes advantage
of the weakness of the kings of Isin and Larsa to assert its independence under *Ilishuma* and *Irishum.* They consider themselves the true bearers of the old Sumerian-Akkadian culture.
They are the only kings who had no foreign blood in their

veins, neither Elamite nor Amorite, and all rulers of their dynasty carry pure Akkadian names. A grandson of Irishum is called *Sharrukin* (Sargon), the same name of the founder of the old Akkadian empire. This may indicate that Assyria, set as guardian of the northern frontier of the land of Akkad, was beginning to mold its foreign policy on the grandiose scheme of Sargon of Agade.

In the eighteenth century B.C. it seemed as if the Elamites would become the sole masters of Mesopotamia. Kudur-Mabug of Yamutbal conquers Larsa and sets as king there his son *Waradsin,* "the servant of Sin." After a brief rule he was succeeded by his younger brother *Rimsin.* In a systematic way he proceeds to annex the neighboring cities. The first to fall into his hands is Uruk. After repeated efforts he triumphs over Isin, the main rival of Larsa. When the goal of complete unification of the land of Sumer and Akkad seemed near at last to Rimsin, *Hammurabi* of Babylon (1728-1686 B.C.) snatches the final triumph from his hands.

Hammurabi of Babylon

It would have been an irony of history should the Elamite Rimsin have established his control over all Mesopotamia, now that the land had been thoroughly permeated with Amorite blood. But even though an Amorite himself, Hammurabi had to fight a long battle against blood-related and foreign kings alike before he was able to unite all of Mesopotamia under his rule. In a few years he conquered Isin, Uruk and part of the territory east of the Tigris. But shifting alliances among the different cities made the work of consolidation extremely difficult. One of his chief rivals was *Shamshi-Adad* I (1748-1717 B.C.) who left Mari to become the ruler of Ashur. From here he expanded his dominion as far as North-Syria and set his son *Yasmah-Adad* "Adad rejoices" as vassal king in Mari. The death of the powerful Shamshi-Adad would have greatly facilitated the task of Hammurabi, were it not for the fact that the weak Yasmah-Adad in Mari was deposed and replaced by *Zimrilin,* a scion of the former dynasty of Mari.

Planted on the banks of the Euphrates, Mari had been an important Amorite center since the beginning of the second millennium. Its imposing ruins have been systematically excavated by the *Musèe de Louvre* since 1933, under the leadership of André Parrot. A temple of Ishtar as well as a ziggurat

The upper part of the Code of Hammurabi. The king is depicted as standing before his god to receive the law from his hand.

Courtesy, the Louvre

have come to light. Most impressive is the royal palace covering fifteen acres, which enclosed not only the royal apartments but administrative offices. From the archives of the palace over twenty thousand tablets were recovered, including the correspondence of Zimrilin with Hammurabi. These documents showed that Shamshi-Adad I was an older contemporary of Hammurabi. Since from the Khorsabad list of Assyrian kings Shamshi-Adad I can be dated about 1747-1717 B.C., further calculations lead to a date for the reign of Hammurabi from 1728 to 1686 B.C. This date is pivotal in the chronology of the ancient Near East. Scholars are not unanimous on the issue, but the weight of evidence seems to favor it. [1]

In his thirty-first year Hammurabi conquered Larsa and captured Rimsin. The following year he conquered Mari which was finally destroyed after a revolt. With this Hammurabi completed the task of territorial expansion, except for minor skirm-

---

1. So W. F. Albright, *BASOR*, 88 (1942), pp. 28-33; P. Van Der Meer, *The Chronology of Ancient Western Asia and Egypt*, p. 35ff.

ishes. The indefatigable monarch could now devote the remaining years of his reign to works of peace which were much closer to his heart.

Hammurabi's ideal of kingship is expressed in the prologue and conclusion of his famous code. He is lord over lands and peoples of the four quarters of the world, but also the pious temple-builder and the shepherd of the black-headed people, the protector of the weak and wronged. He never posed himself as god, nor did he use the divine determinative with his name. Contemporary letters exchanged between Hammurabi and his officials show him as deeply concerned with the welfare of his subjects, interested in every detail of public administration.

Hammurabi's law code, known to scholars since 1902 when it was discovered in Susa, capital of old Elam, by French excavators, is not an original creation as once supposed, but the codification of current Mesopotamian jurisprudence. Earlier law codes have come to light as the one of Urnammu of Ur written in Sumerian, and that of Lipit-ishtar of Isin also in Sumerian. But without question the Code of Hammurabi is the most complete, embodying the main principles of the earlier codes. It is phrased in a typical casuistic style, that is, each separate law states a hypothetical case following it by the appropriate penalty. It stands in contrast to apodictic laws, of which the Mosaic Decalogue is the best example, and which is phrased in the form of commands, such as, "Thou shalt not kill."

The society of Hammurabi's day as reflected in his code is divided into three classes: patricians, plebeians and slaves. The plebeians were bound to the land which they could not sell, or were under some economical obligation to the palace or to a free citizen. Different classes enjoyed different rights under the law. Concerning the family, the code instructs that it was customary for the bridegroom to pay a price to the father of the bride. The bride in turn brings with her a dowry, which on the death of the wife goes to the children, or if she dies childless, returns to the father. Contrary to old Sumerian customs, the wife may get a divorce under certain circumstances and return to her family. The husband may divorce his wife but only under obligation of returning her dowry and additional property. Only marriages concluded by written contract were legally valid. If a man's wife is childless, he may take a concubine which also becomes his legitimate wife. Adoption of children is very common and looms large in Babylonian life. Adopted sons were legal heirs and were expected to perform certain religious duties for the deceased parents.

Harsher than previous Sumerian codes, the code of Hammurabi prescribes the death penalty for calumny, theft, murder, adultery, etc. Fines are imposed in many cases which involved contracts provided they are legally registered. Every commercial transaction was meticulously written by professional scribes, and the names of reliable witnesses attached. Ordeal by water, that is, by throwing the accused into the river, was resorted to when the witnesses to a law suit did not agree.

The Epic of Creation

The two most important pieces of literature from Mesopotamia, the Epic of Creation and the Gilgamesh Epic, which certainly possess a Sumerian nucleus, must have found their classic form in the Akkadian language in the time of Hammurabi. In these epics the old god Enlil of Nippur surrenders the place of honor to Marduk, the local god of Babylon.

The Epic of Creation, often referred to as *Enuma Elish* "When on high," from its opening line, consists of seven tablets describing the triumph of cosmic order over chaos. None of the existing copies is earlier than the first millennium B.C.,

Fragment of the Enuma Elish, Babylonia Creation Story.
Courtesy, British Museum

but considerations of style and content lead to a date in the time of the I dynasty of Babylon. The poem opens with the watery chaos personified by Apsu, the god of the fresh waters, and Tiamat, the goddess of the marine waters. The divine pair begets a numerous progeny of gods which like children eventually disturb the peace of their parents by their untrammeled hilarity. Prompted by the advice of his vizier Mummu, Apsu resolves to destroy his offspring in spite of Tiamat's plea in their behalf. Word goes out among the gods concerning Apsu's plot and dismay fills them. Ea, the all-wise, conceives a counterplot, casts a spell upon Apsu and slays him. At this point the poem introduces the creation of Marduk by Ea, and upon the new god lavish honors are bestowed.

Tiamat is bent to avenge the death of Apsu, and soon she surrounds herself with a hideous entourage of monsters, dragons, vipers, etc. to assist her in her murderous scheme against the gods. She elevates Kingu to be the commander-in-chief of her army. The opposite camp led by Anshar, the forefather of Ea, holds a council of war, and after much discussion chooses Marduk, the hero, to be its champion. The gods confer on Marduk universal kingship and the right to make immutable decrees. Marduk marches to the encounter escorted by the four winds of heaven, the cyclone, the hurricane and the matchless wind, and armed with bow, mace, and most significant of all a net "to enfold Tiamat therein." After a battle call Tiamat and Marduk are locked in single combat. As Tiamat opens her mouth to consume him, Marduk lets loose the winds which fill up Tiamat's belly, "distending her body." He releases the arrow which splits her heart and extinguishes her life. Her cohort of eleven demons together with Kingu are caught in the net and cast into fetters.

Victorious over Tiamat, Marduk splits her body "like a shellfish into two parts." From one he fashions the vault of heaven above and from the other the earth beneath. Of the fifth tablet only a portion is preserved, but there is reason to believe that the missing section dealt with the creation of plants and animals. The sixth tablet narrates the execution of Kingu as promoter of the uprising. Out of Kingu's blood mankind was then fashioned by Ea for "the service of the gods." The poem ends with the designation of Babylon as the abode of the gods and with the ascription of fifty titles of honor to Marduk.

The propaganda purpose of the epic in its present form is evident. Babylon is to be exalted as the mistress of the nations and Marduk as the chief god of its pantheon.

The Epic of Gilgamesh

This epic owes much of its present popularity to the parallel it offers to the Biblical narrative of the flood. The episode of the flood, though, is but a small part of this long poem contained in eleven tablets. Most of the Akkadian texts of the poem come from the library of Ashurbanipal at Nineveh. But that the poem is much older is evinced by the fact that fragments of the epic, both in Akkadian and in Hittite translation dating from the middle of the second millennium, have come to light in the archives of the Hittite empire discovered in Boghazkoy. The original date of the epic may be as much as half a millennium earlier.

The poem sings in the opening stanzas the prowess of the wild hunter Enkidu, and his adopting the charms of civilization through the wiles of a prostitute. In "ramparted Uruk" Enkidu becomes the bosom friend of its king Gilgamesh. Tablet III speaks of the resolve of Gilgamesh to slay the monster Humbaba who resides in the Cedar Forest, while Enkidu does his best to dissuade him. The hero insists on going and is encouraged by dreams as to the outcome of his bout with the giant. Through the broken lines of the text it is possible to visualize Gilgamesh defeating and slaying Humbaba. Tablet VI tells about Ishtar's infatuation at the beauty of Gilgamesh who refuses, though, to become her lover as he recalls the tragic fate of all her previous suitors. Enraged Ishtar asks Anu to send the Bull of Heaven to destroy Gilgamesh. As the bull springs at Enkidu, he thrusts his sword into his neck, slays him, and presents his heart as an offering to their protector Shamash. Enkidu's outrage must be punished and Anu and Enlil decree his death. Enkidu curses his fate until comforted by Shamash he accepts death resignedly.

None weeps more bitterly over Enkidu's death than his friend Gilgamesh, who now stung by the grimness of death sets upon an eventful search for immortality. The hopelessness of his task is made more poignant by the words of a woman who reminds him that, "When the gods created mankind, death for mankind they set aside, life in their own hands retaining." [2] Undaunted Gilgamesh presses on his way now seeking the advice of the Faraway Utnapishtim, counterpart of the Biblical

2. Pritchard, *Ancient Near Eastern Texts*, p. 90, col. I.

Noah, who survived the flood with the help of Ea, and as the only man who had attained immortality now resided at "the mouth of the rivers." In the eleventh tablet, the longest of the series, Utnapishtim recounts to Gilgamesh the instructions he received for the preparation of a boat, the awful storm which brought about the flood, how after seven days the boat came to rest upon Mount Nisir, and how he sent out first a dove, then a swallow, and finally a raven which did not return. As Utnapishtim upon leaving the boat offered a sacrifice, "the gods crowded like flies around the sacrifice." Reproached by the gods for bringing about the deluge and destroying all mankind, Enlil went aboard the ship and bestowed upon Utnapishtim and his wife immortal life.

Completing his story Utnapishtim caused a heavy slumber to fall upon Gilgamesh for seven days. Whereupon Urshanabi who had acted as guide to Gilgamesh is told to wash the hero and equip him for his journey home. At the moment of departure, Utnapishtim persuaded by his wife discloses to Gilgamesh the secret of a plant at the bottom of the sea which would confer him eternal youth. Gilgamesh dives for the plant, brings it back with him, and sets on his homeward journey. Short-lived is his joy, though, for in a moment of neglect a serpent attracted by the scent of the plant emerges from the water and snatches it away. Disconsolate Gilgamesh returns to ramparted Uruk apparently to find comfort in the imperishable wall he built to perpetuate his fame.

Besides epic hymns as the ones described above, Sumero-Akkadian literature abounds with prayers, litanies, rituals, astronomical and mathematical texts, divination formulae, oracles, omina, etc. Business documents are the most numerous and deal with rent contracts, protocols, inventories, administrative records, verdicts and receipts.

Under the successors of Hammurabi, Babylon gradually loses its power. *Shamshuiluna* his son must fight internal revolts and repel an invasion of the Kassites which poured in from the mountains of Luristan. In the south, *Ilumailu* a descendant of the last ruler of the dynasty of Isin succeeds in breaking away from Babylon, founding by the Persian Gulf the Sea-land dynasty, which remains independent for several centuries until destroyed by *Ulamburiash,* the twelfth ruler of the Kassites. Things go from bad to worse until under *Shamshuditana,* the last king of the dynasty, the Hittite Mursilis I conquers Babylon in 1531 B.C. and carries a heavy booty away.

5

THE KASSITE DYNASTY IN BABYLON

After the sack of Babylon, the Kassites who had been gradually and peacefully penetrating Babylonia established their dominion upon the ruins of the empire of Hammurabi. The Kassites, also known to historians as Cossaeans, appear to have come originally from a region near the Caucasus, and from the names of some of their gods it seems that they had been in contact with Indo-Aryan tribes. Possibly the ruling class was Indo-Aryan.

The four hundred years of Kassite domination (c. 1530-1150 B.C.) are years of passivity and political weakness for Babylon. Without a written language, the Kassites finished by forgetting their own and adopting the language of Babylon. The new bloom of the Akkadian literature in this period is a Babylonian and not a Kassite accomplishment. Taking advantage of the growing impotence of the successors of Hammurabi, the Kassites seem to have established an independent kingdom in the northeast of Mesopotamia. Their kings *Gandash, Agum* I, *Kashtiliash* I and II, etc. must be considered as contemporaneous with the last kings of the First Dynasty of Babylon. Only after the plunder of Babylon by the Hittites did *Agum* II occupy the capital with his warriors and make himself king of the whole land. In spite of the evident weakness of the Kassite rulers they keep on using such resounding titles as "king of Sumer and Akkad," "king of the totality," as well as "king of Karanduniash," Karanduniash being the Kassite name for Babylon.

From the "Synchronistic History" found in the library of Ashurbanipal, which narrates the history of Babylon and Assyria in synchronistic parallels, one learns that *Barnaburiash* I, successor of Agum II, negotiated border questions with king *Puzur-ashur* III of Assyria (c. 1490-1470 B.C.). It is also clear from the same source that the Sealand in the south continued independent until the days of *Kashtiliash* III who followed *Barnaburiash* I as ruler of Babylon. His brother Ulamburiash defeated and deposed the last king of the Sealand. When *Ulamburiash* in turn became king of Babylon the whole country was again united.

The subsequent history of the Kassite rule deals with recurring boundary problems with Assyria, diplomatic exchanges with Egypt, and protective measures against the new and powerful kingdom of Mitanni to the northwest. Excavations eleven miles west of Bagdad brought to light the fortress-residence which the Kassite *Kurigalzu* I built about 1400 B.C. in order to strengthen the frontier against Mitanni. With the decline of Mitanni the Kassite kingdom under *Barnaburiash* II (*c*. 1350 B.C.) ranked for a while as third in importance after Egypt and the kingdom of the Hittites. The Amarna archive gives evidence of the exchange of letters and gifts between the Egyptian Akhenaten and the Kassite *Barnaburiash* II both threatened by the ascending might of Suppiluliumas of Hatti.

In the days of the powerful *Tukultininurta* I (*c*. 1250 B.C.) of Assyria, the Kassite *Kashtiliash* IV was defeated and taken prisoner to Ashur. In a second expedition the walls of Babylon were demolished, the treasures of the city and temple plundered, and many Kassites deported to Assyria. Surprisingly the Kassite rulers recovered the throne and enjoyed a relative prosperity for another century while Assyria languished under a series of weak kings. The deathblow to the Kassite dynasty was given by the Elamites who raided Babylon *c*. 1155 B.C., carrying as trophies to Susa, their capital, the law-stela of Hammurabi and the triumph-stela of Naramsin of Agade. With *Enlilnadinahhe* the Kassite dynasty ran its course. The national Babylonian party placed on the throne one of their own thus inaugurating the Second Dynasty of Isin.

Religion

Art during the Kassite period shows a marked tendency to represent the gods by abstract signs rather than in human form. This resistance to the anthropomorphic representation of the deity goes in hand with a stronger stress on the ethical aspect of religion. The "time of trouble" brought upon Babylon by the Kassite rule apparently forced the priesthood to explain why the gods had forsaken the land. A recognition that sin alienated the gods may have imposed itself. From this there was only one step to the conclusion that divine protection may not be enjoyed without a corresponding worthy moral conduct on the part of the people. To every sin must correspond punishment. The next question was also inevitable: Why should the good suffer? This ever-recurrent question is taken up in two literary pieces of the end of the second millennium: one is known by its first line as "Praise to the Lord of Wisdom," and the other as "A Dialogue about Human Misery." Both stress the insufficiency of human morality, and the hopelessness of man's effort to understand the divine way to righteousness.

Disappointingly this striving after ethical excellence is marred by a parallel development of sorcery and demonology. It seems as if people felt themselves beset by demons by day and by night. Priests tried to introduce some order in the dark realm of evil spirits imagining them as subject to the seven evil ones to whom all evil in creation was ascribed. To cope with the ubiquitous threat of demons use was made of set incantations and spells, several collections of which survived as the *Maklu* and *Shurpu* texts. Both words mean "burning," and apparently refer to the rite of burning some object as the spell was pronounced. Magic becomes for the masses of Babylon the only meaningful religion.

Folk Movements of the Second Millennium

The invasion of the Kassites represents only a small fragment of a vast migration of peoples which took place during the second millennium. Another important segment is represented by the Hurrians (Biblical Horites) who press southward from the Armenian Mountains and make their presence felt in North Mesopotamia, Syria and even Palestine, while driving other peoples before them. The mass of the Hurrians seemed to be under the leadership of an Aryan upper class, who called themselves Marianni. In battle they used the horse and the chariot. They gave great attention to horse-breeding. Their most important political organization was the kingdom of Mitanni which flourished in the fifteenth and fourteenth centuries until absorbed into the Hittite empire in the days of Suppiluliumas. The Hurrians show many affinities with the Subarians which also stem from the region of Lake Van. One of the best-known Hurrian sites is Nuzi, where thousands of tablets were discovered by an expedition of Harvard University. Some practices of patriarchal times mentioned in Genesis seem to be related to Nuzian customary law.

6
THE HITTITES

The Hittites had been vaguely known to historians from scanty references, and more recently from allusions in Akkadian texts where their country is named "land of Hatti," or from Egyptian texts of the nineteenth dynasty where there is frequent mention of the "land of Heta." But direct evidence of their existence was brought to light first by Hugo Winckler who carried excavations in Boghazkoy in Turkey from 1906 to 1912. From monumental remains and from thousands of inscriptions in several languages it is possible now to piece together the course of their history.

It is believed the Hittites together with other Indo-Aryan groups migrated from southern Russia early in the second millennium B.C., and after crossing the Caucasus turned westward into Asia Minor. Their language is clearly related to the western group of Indo-European languages. Entering Asia they must have come in contact with the Semites of northern Mesopotamia from whom they learned the cuneiform script, and some of their religious ideas. The Hittites themselves did not form an ethnic unit, but, like the Greeks, were subdivided into many related stems, the Hittites proper with their center about the bow of the Halys River near modern Ankara, the Palaian stems which occupied the region which later came to be called Paphlagonia, and the Luwians in Cilicia.

The history of the Hittites may be divided into three periods: I. The Old Kingdom (1800-1450 B.C.); II. A short Intermediate Period (1450-1400 B.C.); III. The New Empire (1400-1200 B.C.).

The Old Kingdom
The unification of the several Hittite clans under one ruler seems to have been accomplished by *Anittas*. Little else is known

about him and his immediate successors. A tablet which records the law of succession to the throne introduced by king Telipinus begins with a historical preamble typical of Hittite treaties, which mentions as the three outstanding kings of the Old Kingdom, Labarnas, Hattusilis I and Mursilis I.

Labarnas is the real founder of the Hittite kingdom. His name became for all successors on the Hittite throne a title equivalent to king. He strengthened the royal authority in opposition to the nobility. The right to choose a successor which used to be exercised by the council of nobles, the *panku,* passed gradually to the hands of the king himself.

Hittite relief showing a deer hunt. Courtesy, the Louvre

His son *Hattusilis* I is the first Hittite, as far as we know, who embarks on a program of territorial expansion. He tries to annex the principate of Aleppo south of the Taurus Mountains, but without success. Because of intrigues in the court he sets aside his oldest son in behalf of his younger, *Mursilis* I, who was the first to elevate the land of Hatti to the supremacy in the Near East. Mursilis' raid on remote Babylon in 1531 B.C. was unrealistic though, and could not have permanent results. On the other hand he was able to conquer Aleppo, thus avenging his father's defeat. His assassination in a palace conspiracy marked the beginning of a chaotic period in Hittite history. There was no clear right of succession, and conspiracy and murder followed one another. As a result Hittite power sank to its lowest point.

The one to rescue the kingdom from anarchy was king *Telipinus,* a usurper himself, who introduced a constitutional reform clearly defining the right of succession. From his time must also be dated the oldest codification of Hittite law. Telipinus' territorial ambitions were limited to the establishment of a defensible frontier. In this period of Hittite weakness must be reckoned the eighth campaign of Thutmosis III who repelled the Hurrians beyond the Euphrates, and established Egyptian sovereignty in Syria for about thirty years. There is evidence that the Egyptians and Hittites were on friendly terms during the reign of Thutmosis III probably because of the threat posed to both nations by the Hurrians.

The New Empire

The most powerful king of the New Empire is *Suppiluliumas* who takes advantage of Egyptian debility under Akhenaten to annex all the Syrian territory as far south as the river Kelb which flows into the Mediterranean slightly north of modern Beirut. He also subdues all lands of Asia Minor, and conquers the kingdom of Mitanni which had been established in the Upper-Euphrates by the Hurrians. But with prudent self-control he marries his daughter to Mattiwaza, son of Tushratta, the defeated king of Mitanni, and makes of the territory a vassal-state. The far-reaching fame of Suppiluliumas is evinced by the fact that the widow of Pharaoh Tuthankamun dispatches a letter asking him to send one of his sons to become her husband, since she deigned not to marry one of her own subjects. Suppiluliumas complies with the request, but his son was apparently murdered on his arrival in Egypt by an agent of Ai who aspired to the throne himself.

The grandson of Suppiluliumas, *Mursilis* II, is able to preserve for another generation the greatness of the empire, though not without having to fight with enemies on the four points of the compass. To the west the chief enemy is the naval power of the land of Achiyawa, which some historians identify with the Acheans of Greece.

Mursilis' II son, *Muwatallis,* is the one who met Ramesses II of Egypt in the famous battle of Kadesh on the Orontes river, in the year 1296 B.C. In several monumental inscriptions com-memorating the battle Ramesses claims to have won the victory, but the facts favor the conclusion that the battle was indecisive. The Hittites retained their positions in northern Syria, while Egypt is restricted to the south of the river Kelb.

After the death of Muwatallis, his brother *Hattusilis* III broke the right of succession, and usurped the throne from his nephew Urhi-Teshup. So serious was this breach of the law that Hat-tusilis later in life had an autobiography written justifying his act before public opinion. In this remarkable document he ex-plains that he did his very best as a provincial governor to avoid a breach with Urhi-Teshup, but the insolence of the last left him no other alternative than a resort to armed rebellion. Hat-tusilis III brought constant warfare with Egypt to an end by entering into a peace-treaty with Ramesses II. Copies of this treaty are known both from Hittite and Egyptian sources. The original written on a silver tablet has not been discovered. On the other hand Hattusilis could not prevent the vassal-state of Mitanni from falling into the hands of Shalmaneser I of Assyria.

Hattusilis III was the last great king of the Hittites. His suc-cessors must fight against an increasing pressure from the West, until the kingdom was overrun by the invasion of the Sea-peo-ples at the end of the thirteenth century B.C. The Hittites who had a monopoly on the use of iron were defeated by adversaries from the West who also wielded iron weapons. It was the dawn of the Iron Age. Even though the Hittites ceased to exist as a nation in Anatolia, some outposts of Hittite culture survived in northern Syria, and these are the Hittite principalities to which the Old Testament and the Assyrian Annals continue to refer for centuries to come.

Language and Customs

Tablets and monumental inscriptions found in Boghazkoy show that two main languages were used: Hittite proper, an Indo-European language, used for internal administration, and Akkadian which was the language of diplomacy. Tablets in Hur-rian have also been found. Likewise tablets dealing with in-cantations in the Luwian and Palaean dialects have been identi-fied. These two dialects belong to the Indo-European group of languages, and must have been spoken by blood-related tribes. The script employed is either cuneiform which they learned from the Akkadians, or hieroglyphs of a peculiar style preferred for monumental inscriptions. Cuneiform Hittite was first deciphered by the Czech scholar B. Hrozny in 1915 not long after Winckler and Bittel did their pioneer excavations in Boghazkoy.

Hittite society was regulated by a law-code containing about two hundred ordinances of the casuistic type dealing with homicide, marriage, theft, arson, sorcery, etc. Their code gives evidence of development according to changing circumstances, and, in some cases the law is to be applied in harmony with local customs. Disputes were tried before the council of the elders of the city. If a royal officer was stationed in the city he would represent the crown in judicial matters. Provision was made for direct appeal to the king in the case of capital punishment. Careful investigation of the facts seemed to be the rule in judicial disputes as shown in one tablet. Hittite law is remarkable for discountenancing a revengeful spirit. The principle of restitution displaces that of retribution in most cases. Capital punishment is invoked only for rape, sexual intercourse with animals, and civil disobedience. Bodily mutilation is reserved for slaves. In most cases where reparation is prescribed this is in terms of money.

Concerning marriage customs it is to be remarked that the bridegroom normally made a symbolic gift to the family of the bride. At the same time the bride received a dowry from her father. Should the wife die her dowry became the property of her husband, except in the case she still resided in her father's house. Marriage between near relatives was forbidden. In case the husband died childless it was the duty of his brother or nearest kin to marry the widow, the offspring of this union taking the name of the dead man. This finds a close parallel in the levirate marriage prevailing among the Israelites.

The Hittites were polytheistic like all their neighbors. Their gods belonged to several circles: Sumero-Akkadian, West Semitic, native pre-Hittite, and Hurrian. The Hurrian weather-god Teshub with his wife Hebat enjoyed widespread popularity. Equally prominent was the goddess Shaushka identified with the Akkadian Ishtar. She is represented as a winged figure standing on a lion. In the state religion the sun-goddess worshiped in Arinna held first place, being the supreme patroness of the king.

In warfare, since the days of the New Empire, the Hittites relied mainly on the light horse-drawn chariot, as can be seen in the Egyptian reliefs depicting the battle of Kadesh. The Hittite chariots had a crew of three, whereas the Egyptian had

only two. This would give them an advantage when it came
to hand to hand fighting after the first onslaught. For attack
they used the lance and the bow. The infantry played a much
smaller role than the chariotry. Their main duty was to protect the king and the baggage-train. No use was made of cavalry
which did not come to its own until many centuries later.

As seen in the ruins of their capital Hattusas, the Hittites
protected their cities with a double wall. The inner one con-
sisted of an inner and outer shell of masonry with cross-walls
between, the resulting casemates being filled with rubble. Both
walls are strengthened by rectangular towers at intervals of
about one hundred feet. Particular care was taken to protect
the gateways by flanking them with great defensive towers.
Access to the city was by way of a steep ramp along the wall
which made a sharp turn at the entrance, thus exposing any
attacker to maximum surveillance from the walls. In the days
of the New Empire no military action was initiated by the
Hittites without a formal declaration of war, in which the
attacker tried to justify his action before public opinion. If a
city refused to surrender it was stormed, looted and burned to
the ground. The inhabitants would be taken into slavery, but
there is a noticeable absence of the lust for cruelty on which
the Assyrian kings gloated. If an enemy king surrendered peace-
ably he was usually allowed to retain his territory as a vassal
state.

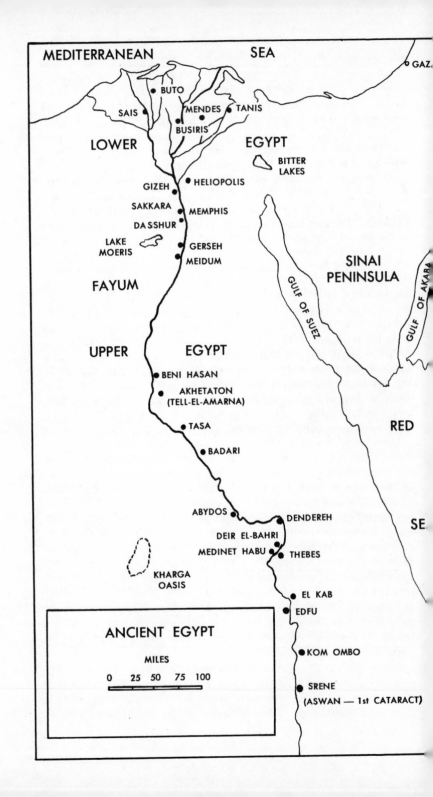

7

PRE-HISTORIC TIMES IN EGYPT

Egypt consists of a long valley never more than a few miles wide which the Nile traverses slowly from south to north over five hundred miles from the first cataract to Memphis. Here near the old capital, approximately where Cairo is located today, the Nile branches forming the fertile Delta which expands into a vast plain as it nears the Mediterranean. Topographically, Egypt is divided into two parts: the long and narrow Upper Egypt, limited on the east and west by mountains bordering on the desert, and the flat Lower Egypt occupying the Delta. This dualism imposed by geography deeply influenced Egyptian history, and is reflected in the native designation for Egypt *tawy*, which means "the two lands."

Herodotus, quoting Hecateus, called Egypt "the gift of the Nile." And so it is indeed, for the regular yearly inundations of the Nile which cover the valley for a few miles on either side of the river is what makes agriculture and settled life possible in a land where rain is practically nonexistent. The inundation begins in June and may last as late as November when the water begins to recede. At its peak the water level at the first cataract may be fifty feet higher than at low water. Tropical rains at the head-waters of the two branches of the Nile are responsible for the yearly inundation and the rich alluvium which restores the fertility of the soil. The arable land in the valley attains a maximum width of ten miles, but its productivity is such that it is one of the most densely populated areas in the world. It is estimated that in Roman times Egypt supported a population of seven million souls.

Since the earliest times man cooperated with the Nile by making canals to carry the water as far as possible from the river, and building water-wheels to lift the water for irrigation of land on higher levels. The regularity of the inundations stimu-

lated man to a more energetic cultivation of the land, the
fertility of which rewarded him proportionately. They taught
man the need of cooperation in the task of digging and maintaining canals and dikes, as well as in the division of the fields
after each inundation erased the land-marks. This need of cooperation led man to live 'in villages, which later on were organized into several nomes or districts. In historical times there
were forty-two nomes, each of which formed also a religious
community attached to the worship of a certain deity, and having its own banner.

Geological evidence points to the fact that the valley of the
Nile was originally covered by ocean water which gradually retreated, but not without leaving clear marks of stratification on
the mountain sides bordering the desert on the east and west.
Following the retreat of the sea, the valley must have been occupied by a dense jungle teeming with animal life. As desiccation
of the adjacent areas progressed, men began to settle on the
edges of the jungle cut by the Nile River. Eventually villages
came into existence, the material remains of which, always more
abundant in the dry south than in the north, have allowed pre-
historians to identify a series of cultures. Corresponding to the Neolithic period the following cultures have been identified mainly
on the basis of artifacts, burial customs, and pottery. In the north:
the Fayum A and B cultures, followed by the Merimde phase,
and this by that of El-Omari; in the south: the Tasa culture. In
the Chalcolithic period the following cultures succeeded each
other: Badari, Amrah and Negade I in the south; Negade II in
the north which finally spread over the whole country. During
the late Negade II traces of contact with Palestine are evident
from the presence of the wave-handle ware in both countries. It
is likely that during this period some West-Semitic group migrated to Egypt whose language made a definite imprint on the
final form of Egyptian. There seems also to have been a cultural
relation between the Jemdet Nasr period of Mesopotamia (c.
3000 B.C.) and the Negade II and early Proto-dynastic of Egypt.
This became particularly clear from excavations in Tell Judeideh
in the region of the Delta, where brick tombs with niched walls
and cylinder seals with peculiar designs were found. The inter-
twined serpents on the palette of king Narmer also reveal a
typical Mesopotamian motif.

Documentary Sources of Egyptian History

The division of Egyptian history into thirty dynasties is the work of Manetho, an Egyptian priest who lived in the third century B.C. None of his writings have survived, except as quoted by Josephus, and some Christian writers, particularly Africanus. Africanus in turn survived mainly through Eusebius, whose works are preserved in Latin and Armenian.

Manetho may have used some priestly traditions and primary sources some of which are known to modern historians. Among these are the following:

(a) Turin Papyrus — originally contained a complete list of kings from Menes down to Ramesses II.

(b) Palermo Stone — mentions kings of the Old Kingdom as well as the level of the Nile for different years.

(c) Abydos king list — carved on the walls of a temple in Abydos it presents Sethos I worshiping his ancestors, seventy-seven of which are named.

(d) Karnak king list — shows Thutmosis III worshiping his ancestors, of which sixty-one are named.

(e) Saqqara Tablet — so-called because it was found in a tomb in Saqqara, mentions forty-seven kings down to Ramesses II.

Other sources are biographies preserved in tombs. Particularly valuable are biographies of persons who lived through more than one reign, which then allows us to know something of the sequence of kings. So from the tomb of the official Martet-ites we have a list of titles related to Snefru, Khufu and Khafre all pharaohs of the Fourth Dynasty. In the case of Ptah-shepsis it is possible to deduce a link between the Fourth and Fifth Dynasties from the autobiography carved on the wall of his tomb. Certain monumental inscriptions are also valuable sources of information for the historian as those of the campaigns of Tuthmosis III, or of Ramesses II. Scarabs may be instructive for frequently they contain the title of the reigning monarch which helps to identify and date the site in which it was found. Amenophis III, for example, had many scarabs made to commemorate among other things his marriage to a Mitannian princess.

Chronology of Egypt

The greatest single contribution to the clarification of Egyptian chronology was the work of the German historian Eduard Meyer, who published his results in 1904. He was the first to point out the importance of the Sothic Cycle for Egyptian Chronology.

By Sothic Cycle we understand the interval of 1460 years between two coincidences of the civil and Sothic year. Early in their history the Egyptians must have found by averaging the intervals between many successive inundations of the Nile that the year had 365 days. Accordingly they adopted a calendar of twelve months of thirty days each, to which they added five days at the end of the year. This was their civil year. The Sothic year which is the interval between two successive early risings of the star Sirius (Sothis in Greek) just prior to sun-rising, corresponds to an astronomical year of roughly 365¼ days. This means that the civil year fell short of the astronomical year at the rate of one day every four years, and therefore 365 days, or a full year, every 1460 years. The beginning of the civil year and that of the astronomical year as measured by the star Sothis would coincide at the end of every Sothic cycle. The Roman writer Censorinus registered one such coincidence in what corresponds to the year A.D. 137. Figuring back it is calculated that other coincidences would correspond to the years 1317, 2772 and 4225 B.C. References to the early rising of Sothis in relation to the civil year, as found in some Egyptian papyri, allow us to calculate the exact date of such occurrence with the help of the dates above. One such reference is found on the Ebers Papyrus from the beginning of the Eighteenth Dynasty. Another is found in the Illahun Papyrus which refers to a heliacal rising of Sirius on the fifteenth day of the eighth month of the seventh year of Sesostris III, a pharaoh of the Middle Kingdom. That date may then be exactly calculated thus furnishing an absolute date for the reign of Sesostris III (1878-1841 B.C.).

Divisions of Egyptian History

The classification of the Egyptian kings into thirty dynasties was the work of Manetho, but his scheme is still followed by most historians. The following table presents a synoptic view of Egyptian history according to period, dynasties and respective dates.

Period	Dynasties	Dates
Protodynastic	I — II	c. 2850-2650
Old Kingdom	III — VI	c. 2650-2150
First Intermediate Period	VII — X	c. 2150-2050
Middle Kingdom	XI — XII	c. 2050-1780
Second Intermediate Period	XIII — XVII	c. 1780-1570
The New Empire	XVIII — XXIV	c. 1570-708
Period of Decline	XXV — XXX	708-332

8

PROTO-DYNASTIC PERIOD AND
THE OLD KINGDOM

On the threshold of historical times the districts of Upper Egypt were united under one king and so were those of Lower Egypt. The crown used by monarchs of Upper Egypt was a tall white helmet, that of Lower Egypt was a red wickerwork diadem. The names of some of these kings appear in a fragment of the Palermo Stone. Eventually the two parts of the land were united under one king who used the double crown of Upper and Lower symbolic of a united country. According to the tradition found in old religious texts, united Egypt broke up again into its two natural divisions which were ruled by kings known as "worshipers of Horus." The double capitals, one representing the political and the other the religious center, were Nechab and Nechen (modern Elkab south of Luxor) in Upper Egypt, and Dep and Pe (Buto of Greek times) in Lower Egypt. This period can not be long since the tomb finds of the late Negade II culture are followed without break in style by those of the First dynasty.

The last king of Upper Egypt is known as king "Scorpion" from inscriptions found on monuments in Hierankopolis. Closest stylistically to the monuments of king "Scorpion" are those of king *Narmer*. From the monuments one concludes that Narmer is the oldest and first ruler who carried both crowns. Representations on his ceremonial slate palette shows that as ruler of Upper Egypt he had annexed Lower Egypt, thus uniting the country once more. Many historians are inclined to identify Narmer with *Menes,* who according to Herodotus was the founder of the First Dynasty. But the fact is that the name of Menes appears only once on monuments of the early dynastic period, and namely as Nebti-name of a king whose Horus-name was Aha. One must remember that in the royal titulature the

Pharaoh was given five names of which the Horus name was the first and the Nebti name the second. The third name was the Golden Horus name, the fourth was the one following the title "king of Upper and Lower Egypt," and the fifth the name

Narmer palette in the
Cairo Museum.
Courtesy, S. H. Horn

211

following the epithet "son of Re." It is quite possible that *Aha,* "fighter," was the name which Narmer assumed after conquering Lower Egypt. Another alternative is that Narmer could not long enjoy his victory over Lower Egypt, and therefore the glory of uniting permanently the country went to his immediate successor *Aha-Menes.*

Herodotus attributes to Menes the founding of Memphis, the capital of the Old Kingdom, together with that of the temple of Ptah, where the bull Apis was worshiped. He surrounded the capital with a great, white wall. The old capital was located south of modern Cairo on the west bank of the Nile. Its location near the point where the Nile branches into the Delta remained a strategic point throughout Egyptian history. The tomb of Aha (Menes) was found in a cemetery on the desert near the village of Saqqara. But the other kings of the first two dynasties had their tombs near Abydos (Thinis) in Upper Egypt, which was the place of origin of their ancestors. For this reason the first two dynasties are called Thinite Dynasties by Eduard Meyer. The Thinite kings stressed their southern origin by always placing in the double symbolism of Egypt the symbols of Upper Egypt first: the vulture before the uraeus (cobra), the rush before the bee or the papyrus, the white crown before the red, etc., which became normative for all times. This attachment to Upper Egypt explains why all kings of the First Dynasty except the first had their tombs built in Abydos. Even though robbed in ancient times, these tombs have rewarded the modern excavator with many treasures worthy of their royal possessors.

The style of the royal tombs of this dynasty, as Petrie has shown, bears direct relation to those of the late Negade II culture. The access to the funeral chamber is gained by a staircase, and the main chamber is surrounded by smaller ones where the royal entourage was buried. The tomb of the last king of the First Dynasty, that of *Kea,* gives evidence that people were buried in the lateral chambers at the same time that the royal remains were placed in the main chamber. If so, this would be a repetition of the custom also found to prevail later in Ur of Mesopotamia, where according to Woolley courtiers killed themselves or were put to death in order to accompany the king to the nether-world.

There are references from the First Dynasty to skirmishes with the bedouins in the Sinai Peninsula caused by the desire of the pharaohs to take possession of the mines of malachite from which copper was extracted. The semi-precious turquoise was also mined in the same area. Sinai remained through the centuries the main source of copper for Egypt. Kings who led expeditions to Sinai were wont to make reliefs on the rocks commemorating their exploits. The oldest of these shows king *Semerkhet* (Greek Semempses), the next to the last king of the First Dynasty, in the act of clubbing to death a bedouin.

Commercial relations were carried with Byblos on the Phoenician coast, not far north from modern Beirut, from where the Egyptians imported the precious cedar-wood. There is also evidence of exchange of goods with Crete in this early period.

Of the kings of the Second Dynasty only two tombs were found in Abydos, namely those of *Peribsen* and *Chasechemui.* Peribsen was a heretic who replaced the worship of Horus which prevailed in Lower Egypt by that of Seth, who was the chief god in Upper Egypt since immemorial times. The tomb of Chasechemui is the first to show a main funerary chamber built of well cut limestone blocks, whereas the rest of the funerary installation is made of bricks as usually.

The Old Kingdom

From the Third Dynasty on, the hegemony of Lower Egypt becomes undisputed for the remainder of the Old Kingdom period. Also from this time on all rulers have their tombs near Memphis.

King *Djoser* (Zoser) is the first king of the Third Dynasty which comprises only four kings, and did not last more than fifty-five years. Little is known about king Djoser except that he built for himself the now famous step-mastaba of Saqqara, also known as the step-pyramid. Reaching the height of 204 feet and built completely of stone, it became the proto-type of future pyramids. Erected on the border of the desert west of Memphis, Djoser's pyramid was originally surrounded by a white wall just like Memphis itself. In fact the belief seemed to prevail that the king continued to enjoy his royal prerogatives in the other life. The tomb chamber proper was excavated deep in the ground under the massive step-mastaba.

The architect of this monumental tomb was Imhotep, one of the most distinguished builders of antiquity. Centuries later Imhotep was revered by his countrymen as a saint and patron of the scribes. The Greeks who settled in Egypt in later times called him Imuthes and identified him with Asklepios, the god of medicine.

Little is known of the military prowess of the kings of the Third Dynasty except that they conquered part of Nubia south of the first cataract. There is a triumphal stela of king Djoser in Sinai, but it sheds little light upon the historical situation.

Snefru is reckoned as founder of the Fourth Dynasty. He is thought to have come from Lower Egypt. With him we enter the age of the great pyramids. Three pyramids of monumental proportions seem to have been built by Snefru. The first one erected at Medum was never finished and gives today the appearance of a three-step pyramid. The second is the "Bent Pyramid" at Dashur, so called because an error of construction resulted in a sharp angle in the middle of the pyramid. The third, the "Red Pyramid," attained the impressive height of 330 feet, and must be considered the oldest perfect pyramid.

Only a thorough investigation will show under which one lies the actual tomb of the king.

Cheops (Egyptian Khufu) became renowned as the builder of the largest pyramid at Giza. This measured 756 feet on each side at the base, and attained a height of 481 feet. More than two million blocks of stone weighing two and a half tons in the average were required. The engineering skill of the builders is almost unbelievable considering they had no surveying instruments. Even so the angles at the base are almost exactly 90°; the difference between the longest and the shortest side is only nine inches, and the orientation of the pyramid on the four points of the compass is nearly perfect. Originally the pyramid had a revetment of lime-stone still visible near the apex.

For religious reasons the pyramids were built on the western fringe of the desert. The stones were quarried in the mountains to the east of the Nile opposite to Giza. From there the stone blocks were dragged a few miles to the banks of the Nile at the time of the inundation, ferried across the river on barges, and dragged again along especially built ramps to the building perimeter on the west. The complete religious installation of a pyramid comprised: the "portal" where the barges had landed, the ramp now transformed into a covered "processional street," the "funerary temple" where the last rites were performed, and the pyramid proper under which lay the royal tomb. Access to the tomb was through shafts, the entrances to which were carefully concealed. In spite of all precautions, scarcely a royal tomb escaped the cupidity of robbers, which in some cases began their activity soon after the burial ceremonies were over. The massive tombs intended to preserve the safety of the royal mummies proved in the end a colossal failure.

Throughout most of the Old Kingdom it was customary for the nobles to build their mastaba tombs in the vicinity of the royal pyramid as a means of ensuring their survival as attendants of the king. In the First Intermediate Period when the prestige of the king declined sharply, and skepticism concerning the divinity of the sovereign was widespread, nobles returned to the custom of building their tombs near the place where they lived.

Little else is known about the twenty-five year reign of Cheops, or, for that matter, about any of his successors, except that they built pyramids. But this single fact made the names of *Cheops, Chefren* and *Mykerinos* (Egyptian Menkaure) famous for all time.

Chefren, a son of Cheops and builder of the second largest pyramid, did not follow his father on the throne, but was preceded by *Dedefre* to whom eight years are ascribed. Dedefre married a daughter of Cheops, Hetep-heres, which from a painting in the tomb of her daughter appears as blond with blue eyes, and dressed in foreign fashion. She is the oldest known representative of the so-called blond Libyan, and points to the fact that Cheops himself must have married a blond Libyan. The pyramid of Dedefre has vanished, except for a staircase leading into the underground burial chamber.

The last king of the dynasty *Shepses-kaf*, probably a son of Mykerinos, built his tomb at Saqqara, but not in the form of a pyramid. The installation known today as "Mastaba el-Fara'un" had the form of a two-step mastaba, or better, of a gigantic cenotaph with vaulted deck.

To the Fourth Dynasty, besides the six kings above mentioned, Manetho added three more, the names of which are neither mentioned in the kings' lists nor on any monument. They must have been, at best, local rulers or rival kings of short duration. The six kings of the Fourth Dynasty would have ruled approximately from 2600-2480 B.C.

The transition from the Fourth to the Fifth Dynasty was mediated by a queen, Hentkaus, probably a daughter of

Sphinx with stela of Thutmosis IV and Chefren's pyramids.
Courtesy, S. H. Horn

Mykerinos, who married *User-kaf,* the founder of the Fifth Dynasty. As for the previous dynasties, there is little historical information concerning the Fifth. From the names of the kings the majority of which show the component *Re,* one concludes that the worship of the sun-god enjoyed wide popularity. Relief scenes found in the funerary temples, even though not very illuminating concerning historical facts, allow us to recognize the foreign peoples with which Egypt had contact: bedouins of Sinai, the inhabitants of Phoenicia, the brown Libyans of the west, and the Nubians of the south. Egypt was not so closed to outside influences as some times imagined. Only three pyramids of the kings of the Fifth Dynasty are known, namely those of *Sahure, Neferirkare* and *Neuserre.* They are all located in Abusir south of Giza, and are all much smaller than those of the Fourth Dynasty. According to the data furnished by the kings' lists, the Fifth Dynasty ruled approximately 130 years (*c.* 2480-2350).

According to the same sources, the last king of the Fifth Dynasty was *Unas* (Egyptian Unis). Some historians reckon him among the kings of the Sixth Dynasty because his pyramid has, in common with those of this dynasty, inscriptions of a religious nature in some of the chambers and passages. These inscriptions are known as Pyramid Texts and constitute the best primary source for the study of ancient Egyptian religious thought. The names of the kings of this dynasty are *Teti, Pepi* I (Phios), *Merenre, and Pepi II* (Phiops). Their pyramids lie at Saqqara, south of the step-mastaba of Djoser of the Third Dynasty, and are all very modest. The material resources of the realm had been drained by the expensive funeral installations.

The kings' lists ascribe ninety years to the reign of Pepi II. Inscriptions from his time allow us to perceive a deterioration of the royal power. A contemporary document, known from a manuscript of the Eighteenth Dynasty, paints the situation under a very old and inactive king during whose rule the social and political order was breaking down. Upper Egypt makes itself independent from Memphis, and hordes of foreigners move from the Sinai Peninsula into Lower Egypt.

The Seventh Dynasty, which according to Manetho had seventy kings which together ruled seventy days, must be considered fictitious. The Eighth Dynasty comprised eighteen kings whose rule must have been limited to Memphis and immediate vicinity. The Turin Papyrus counts the kings of the Sixth and Eighth Dynasties together and ascribes to them 181 years. It makes thereafter a great break, as if to indicate that with these a major period of Egyptian history was closed.

Administrative Aspects of the Old Kingdom

Egypt appears during the Old Kingdom as an absolute monarchy. The king is the center and soul of the state. For the Egyptian people the king is a god on earth, the incarnation of Horus. The kissing of the king's foot is mentioned as an exceptional honor in a tomb inscription. The construction of a pyramid as the last resting place of the pharaoh, even though of colossal proportions, must not be interpreted as imposing on the common people a tyrannical burden. For the believing Egyptian it was a religious duty gladly performed. Cheops, the builder of the greatest pyramid of all, was not, as far as we can see, dreaded by the people as a tyrant. On the contrary, for many centuries people of all stations in life were anxious to build their tombs near that of the great king. Nearest to the pyramid were the mastabas of relatives of the king and of those who were honored with the title of *rech-nesw*, "acquaintance of the king." Later this title was appropriated by any commoner as a kind of a magical spell. To provide funerary offerings of bread, beer, meat, etc. for the ones honored with a mastaba near the royal tomb, the king endowed them with the revenue of some village which eventually became the private property of the family of the deceased. Thus the notion of private property spread out, whereas originally all land was considered property of the king.

During the Fourth Dynasty the kingdom presents the picture of a strong centralized state, with the administrative offices in Memphis. To fill positions in the civil service sons of prominent families were educated in the court together with the royal princes. The initiation in the civil service was the office of scribe. This very common title should be understood as referring to any public officer. The highest position was that of the vizier, who acts as prime minister. Commerce flourished during most of this period, the main avenue of trade being the Nile itself which swarmed with barges north- and southbound. It was not uncommon for a foreign vessel bringing merchandise from Byblos or Crete to dock at Memphis. Taxes were paid in kind, there being large storehouses for hoarding the government revenue in every major town. A census of the cattle was taken every two years, and official estimates were made of the prospective crops to figure revenues. Humorous bas-relief scenes show that the citizenry was not any more anxious to pay taxes then as now. Weights of stone with engraved units have been found in different sites.

During the Sixth Dynasty there is a slacking of the strong centralized administration. The provinces tend to become autonomous. The nomes originally governed by appointees of the king by and by become hereditary. Nomarchs no longer feel bound to have their tombs built near that of the pharaoh in Memphis. While submissive to the crown as long as the royal power was strong, the nomarchs tend more and more to assert their independence. The Old Kingdom at its close clearly dissolves itself into a feudal society.

Religion in the Old Kingdom

The Pyramid Texts portray the pharaohs of the heydays of the Old Kingdom as departing to heaven where they resume their divine life. Popular imagination embellished this journey depicting the king as flying to heaven either as a goose or a falcon, or ascending a celestial stairway. He was then identified with Re, taking his place in the solar bark with which he daily traversed the sky.

Any attempt to classify the Egyptian gods into groups is bound to meet defeat since the Egyptians were not systematic at all in their religious beliefs. The classification of gods according to whether they were worshiped in Upper or Lower Egypt, or whether they were represented in animal or human form, or with a human body with an animal head, stumbles over many exceptions. Even cosmic deities which would be expected to be portrayed in human form are at times depicted in animal form. So the sky-goddess Nut is depicted both as a woman and as a cow, and the sun-god Horus is represented both by a falcon and by a falcon-headed man wearing the sun disk as a crown. Among the minor deities represented in purely animal form are the following: Sobek as a crocodile; Thot of Hermopolis, the god of wisdom, as an ibis; Khnum in the form of a ram; the bad god Seth as a griffin.

The town of Heliopolis in Lower Egypt developed in historical times a solar religion at the head of which stood the sun-god Re usually represented by the solar disk. Re was at times associated with the local god of Heliopolis, Atum, as a single deity with the title Re-Atum. In the frame of this Heliopolitan religion, the pharaoh was conceived as the son of Re, this concept finding expression in the fifth name of the royal titulature.

A further development in the theology of the priests of Heliopolis is the establishment of a hierarchy among the gods. Thus we read of the "great ennead," the nine gods of their pantheon, at the head of which stood Atum, who brought to existence the god Shu (air) and the goddess Tefnet. From the marital intercourse of these were born Geb (earth) and Nut (heaven), in turn parents of the two pairs, Osiris and Isis, Seth and Nephthys. In a later myth Horus was conceived as the son of Osiris and Isis, and the avenger of Osiris who had been murdered by his brother Seth.

On the other hand the priests of Memphis conceived another "ennead" headed by Ptah, the creator and source of the other deities. Atum is fourth in rank but still recognized as the one through whose word everything was created. In spite of the apparent contradiction, Ptah remains as the creator since he is thought as living in every god, man and beast. The reader must beware of any sweeping generalization when dealing with Egyptian religion, since the Egyptians themselves were never concerned in ironing out discrepancies in their different concepts of the ultimate reality. All approaches might be equally valid in their thinking.

The dominant preoccupation with the after-life is evident in their elaborate preparations for burial. At first a simple tomb in the sand at the edge of the desert towards the west was good enough. Later the tomb was walled with bricks, while on top at the level of the ground a small funeral chapel was erected where offerings for the dead were wont to be brought. Eventually mastabas, bench-like tombs made of bricks or dressed stones, were considered the appropriate thing for the nobility, while kings beginning with Djoser of the Third Dynasty spent fortunes building pyramids.

To ensure the safe passage of the king to the beyond the custom was adopted of inscribing religious texts, mainly prayers and incantations, on the walls of the corridors and funerary chambers of the pyramids.

The Egyptian belief in life beyond the tomb was intimately associated with the notion of a soul which survived in the hereafter. The soul was thought to fly about freely in the world, but would return to the safety of the tomb at night. In order to enable it to recognize the body of its owner great pains were taken to preserve the body from decomposition. Hence the custom arose of embalming the body. The *ka* was not the soul but a kind of tutelary spirit born with the individual, a sort of

doublet. In later relief scenes in tombs it was represented as a
bird fluttering in the air or a bird with a human head. It
escaped death and carried on its protective role in the after-life.

9

FIRST INTERMEDIATE PERIOD

As stated in the last chapter during the long reign of Pepi II royal power declined considerably in Egypt. Many nomarchs acted independently, and tomb inscriptions show that there were constant struggles for supremacy among them. There are traces of a dynasty from Koptos and another from Abydos which were unable, though, to impose rule over all of Egypt for any length of time.

The Egyptians themselves considered the nomarchs of Herakleopolis as the true successors of the Pharaohs of the Old Kingdom, and they are counted in the kings' lists as the Ninth and Tenth Dynasties. Their capital, Herakleopolis, lay in the vicinity of the modern Fayum, and they were able to annex Memphis to their territory. Burial customs, such as the offering of models of ships and granaries for the use of the deceased in the afterlife, show that there was no sharp break with the past.

The founder of the Ninth Dynasty was the nomarch Cheti (Greek Achtoes), who made Memphis the capital once more. He did not rule over all of Egypt, though. South of Abydos and as far as the first cataract ruled the nomarchs of Thebes, who eventually would found the Eleventh Dynasty. According to Winlock who did more than any one to clarify the history of this period, the overthrow of the Herakleopolitan dynasty by the Thebans took place in 2052 B.C. What the distinction is between the Ninth and Tenth Dynasties is not clear. Some believe the Tenth Dynasty had its root in Hermopolis. To this dynasty belong king *Achtoes* III, and his son and successor *Merikare*, known from the literary work, "Teaching for King Merikare," which embodies the political advice given him by his father.

Little is known about the political events of the First Intermediate Period which covers approximately the interval between 2150 and 2052 B.C. On the other hand this time of trouble which wrenched Egyptian life out of its traditional moorings produced the highest flowering of literature in its existence as a nation. The social revolution which took place during this period of upheaval is well reflected in the "Lamentation of Ipur-wer," which is thought to describe conditions prevailing during one of the last kings of the Sixth Dynasty or shortly thereafter. The following excerpts are typical of this literary composition:

> Why really, poor men have become the possessors of treasures. He who could not make a pair of sandals is now the possessor of riches . . . Why really, nobles are in lamentation, while poor men have joy. Every town says: "Let us banish many from us."
> Behold, he who was buried as a falcon (now lies) on a (mere) bier. What the pyramid hid has become empty.
> Behold now, it has come to a point where the land is despoiled of the kingship by a few irresponsible men.1

The political chaos brought about a deep pessimism and a down-grading of the concept of the divinity of the king. Parallel to this is to be seen a growing feeling of individual responsibility before God which led to a greater emphasis on moral conduct. From the "Teaching for King Merikare" it is clear that every man is thought responsible before a divine judgment for his conduct on earth.

> Do justice whilst thou livest upon earth. Quiet the weeper; do not oppress the widow; supplant no man in the property of his father . . . More acceptable is the character of one upright of heart than the ox of the evildoer.2

To the same period belongs also the original of the "Eloquent Peasant." A peasant who had been arbitrarily robbed by an officer makes a series of eloquent pleas before an indifferent judge until he obtains justice. It reflects the high regard with which eloquence was held in Egypt. Perhaps the most interesting product of this age of pessimism and skepticism is the "Dialogue of a Man with his Soul." A man weary of life contemplates suicide as a means of escape to a happier existence. The soul protests with the affirmation that it is better to enjoy this present life since no one is sure of the next. From this composition we transcribe the following famous lines:

> Death is in my sight today (like) the recovery of a sick man, like going out into the open after a confinement. Death is in my sight today like

---

1. Pritchard, *Ancient Near Eastern Texts,* p. 441ff.
2. *Ibid.,* p. 414ff.

the odor of myrrh, like the sitting under an awning on a breezy day . . . Death is in my sight today like the longing of a man to see his house (again) after he has spent many years held in captivity.[3]

To the same class belongs the "Song of the Harper," of which several copies from the New Kingdom are known.

Another development traceable to the First Intermediate Period is the growing popularity of the cult of Osiris, the god of the dead, who as judge dwells in the netherworld and who gives the sentence of life or death at the judgment. The prevailing religious ideas can be gathered from the "Coffin Texts" which are an outgrowth of the "Pyramid Texts." But whereas the latter were intended to benefit only the king, the "Coffin Texts" contain prayers, incantations and confessions in behalf of any mortal. The religion of Osiris with its idea of a final judgment might have worked for a higher moral conduct of all society. But unhappily it did not lead to this result, because Osiris did not remain as the unattainable model for all men, whom mortals would strive to emulate. On the contrary, the belief soon spread that any mortal might be just as blameless as Osiris himself. According to a popular myth, Osiris had been murdered by his brother Seth, and even after his resurrection by the intervention of Isis and Horus, was again accused by Seth before the gods. He convinced the judges of his innocence and was declared "true of voice," that is, "justified." By and by every mortal appropriated for himself the appelative "true of voice," which in the long run came to mean merely "deceased." It is to lament that the beautiful ethical principles expressed in the literature of the Harakleopolitan time were soon stifled by the dry formalism of the religion of Osiris and brought no fruition.

The popular cult of Osiris thrived side by side with the state religion of Re which after its first bloom in the Fifth Dynasty had a new spurt of life in the First Intermediate Period. From this time stem such double divine appelatives as Khnum-Re, Sobek-Re, etc. Most famous of these double appelatives is that of Amun-Re in which Re is identified with Amun, the wind-god of Thebes. Amun-Re attains his maximum popularity in the days of the Eighteenth Dynasty, in which Thebes basked in royal favor. The ascendancy of Amun-Re, usually explained by purely political reasons, should be sought in the simple realization that the sun and the air are the chief creative forces in nature.

Monumental inscriptions from this period are rather scarce.

---

3. *ANET*, p. 405-407.

Much more helpful to clarify the historical situation are the stamp-seals which replaced the roll-seals in a country where writing on papyrus was much more common than on clay tablets. The most common of the stamp-seals is the scarab which first appears in the Sixth Dynasty. The scarab is a stamp-seal carved· in the form of a beetle sacred to the Egyptians as the symbol of the resurrection. Thousands of scarabs have been collected throughout Egypt, and even in tombs in Palestine where they were used as amulets. Since they often have engraved on them the name of the reigning monarch, they are helpful in dating the site where they are found, besides giving an idea of the prevailing artistic motifs of the period.

10
THE MIDDLE KINGDOM

Thebes and the Eleventh Dynasty

The reunification of Egypt was the accomplishment of the nomarchs of Thebes, the main city of the fourth nome, which thus far had played no part in Egyptian history. The chief deity of the nome was the war-god Montu represented with a falcon's head, whose main sanctuary was in Hermonthis. From the tomb-inscriptions of some of these nomarchs, it is clear that besides their proper name Intef they used a Horus name as the king of the oldest times, thus claiming the right to rule Egypt in opposition to the Herakleopolitan kings of the Tenth Dynasty who resided in Memphis. *Intef* IV began in earnest the fight against the Tenth Dynasty, and was able to conquer the eighth nome where Thinis and Abydos lay, and push his control as far as the tenth nome. King *Achtoes* III of the Tenth Dynasty succeeded in reconquering Thinis, but in his instructions to his son Merikare he betrays ignorance of the real threat posed by the south to the hegemony of his house. Soon after, the Theban king *Mentuhotep* II/III conquered Herakleopolis, and brought all of Egypt under his rulership. According to Winlock, whose investigations threw much light on this period, the date of this event was 2052 B.C., and from this time on the Eleventh Dynasty was in full control.

Since the Illahun Papyrus with its reference to a Sothis-date allows us to fix astronomically the seventh year of Sesostris III of the Twelfth Dynasty as the year 1871 B.C., and since the regnal years of the kings of the Twelfth Dynasty are well known, Winlock was able to figure the year 1991 B.C. as the date for the beginning of the Twelfth Dynasty. Reckoning back from this fixed date, Winlock, on the basis of the data of the Turin Papyrus, calculated the year 2134 B.C. as the date for the inauguration of the Eleventh Dynasty. But as we have stated before, the Eleventh Dynasty was only able to assert its rule over a unified Egypt from 2052 B.C. on. The credit for this goes to Mentuhotep II/III whose name was revered for centuries as founder of the Theban Kingdom, and he is represented in tombs of the New Kingdom as a kind of "saint of the necropolis."

The only great monument left by the Eleventh Dynasty is the imposing tomb installation of king Mentuhotep in the valley of Der el-Bahari in the northern section of the Theban west-side. After the reunification of the country it must have been felt that it was necessary for the new Theban kings, like their predecessors in Memphis during the Old Kingdom, to build tombs commensurate with their new dignity. But whereas pyramids were impressive enough in the relatively flat countryside near Memphis, they would be inconspicuous in a mountain region as the one near Thebes where the cliffs may rise to a height of fifteen hundred feet. So the architects of Mentuhotep conceived the idea of building a funerary temple surrounded with a colonnade, and to set on top of this a pyramid of modest proportions. Nothing but ruins are left of the whole complex, but relief scenes of the old temple found on the spot show a peculiar style. Unheard of in the whole of Egyptian royal representations are scenes showing the king very informally in the company of his concubines. From Gebelen, eighteen miles south of Thebes, come two reliefs which celebrate the victories of king Mentuhotep. On one the king is portrayed, in the traditional fashion, in the act of killing a Libyan chieftain, and on the other in the act of killing an Egyptian, a Nubian, an Asiatic, and a Libyan. It is also to be remarked that in this relief scene the pharaoh is portrayed as using only the white crown of Upper Egypt. These scenes are indicative of the struggle for power that went on in Egypt before the Eleventh Dynasty was able to assert its supremacy.

Mentuhotep had a fifty-one year reign, of which forty-two years as ruler of all Egypt. He was followed by his son *Seankhkare-Mentuhotep,* who ruled twelve years. The fact that no burial-place of his has been identified leads historians to conclude that with him the Eleventh Dynasty came to an unhappy end.

As the nobles during the Old Kingdom used to build their mastaba tombs near the pyramids of the pharaohs, so now the nobles have their tombs excavated on the mountain-side surrounding the pyramid installation of king Mentuhotep at Der el-Bahari. Particularly notable is the tomb of the vizier Mektire because of the rich find of painted wood models discovered in it, which depict many aspects of contemporary Egyptian life, such as, activities of the crew on a boat sailing on the Nile, men kneading dough, women straining beer, etc.

From this period dates the earliest collection of the so-called Execration Texts. True to Egyptian belief in magic, it was customary to write the name of an enemy on a vessel together with a curse, and then break the vessel in a consecrated place or a tomb. By this act it was believed the curse would become efficacious against the person so accursed. By collating many pieces together with unending patience, the German scholar Sethe was able to recover complete texts of curses. These are addressed first of all against the traditional enemies of Egypt like the Nubians and the Asiatic. But some are directed against individual Egyptians as can be seen from their names. Among these are the names of Amenemhet and Senwosret (Sesostris), which are the most common names of kings of the Twelfth Dynasty. Since the Turin Papyrus has a note concerning a seven-year period of confusion at the end of the Eleventh Dynasty, we may rightly conclude that the Eleventh Dynasty ended up in a bitter contest for power.

The Twelfth Dynasty

The Twelfth Dynasty is the first in the long series of dynasties the dates for which can be fixed with precision, thanks to the Sothis date from the seventh year of Sesostris III. Besides the duration of every single reign is well known from the Turin Papyrus. It held power for 213 years. Its first king was *Amenemhet* I who took the precaution to associate with him as coregent his son, shortly before his death. The rather common quarrels over succession to the throne brought about by a king's death is reflected in the famous "Story of Sinuhe" which portrays conditions at the death of Amenemhet I. His son and coregent *Sesostris* I who was engaged in a military campaign in the Libyan frontier, on hearing of the death of his father, secretly rushed back to the court so as to assure the throne to himself. Sinuhe who occupied a high position in the army thinking he might have given occasion for the new king to doubt his loyalty fled into voluntary exile in Asia where he spent many eventful years. In his old age he was recalled to the court and cumulated with honors. It is thought that the land of Yaya where "wine was more plentiful than water" stands for Syria whose hospitality Sinuhe praises in his story.

The two names Amenemhet and Sesostris which alternate as royal names of the Twelfth Dynasty mean respectively, "Amun is at the head," and "the man of the (goddess) Wosret." These theophoric names show that the god Montu so popular during the preceding dynasty had been replaced by Amun, who from now on stands at the head of the Egyptian pantheon. Later it was identified with the sun-god Re and worshiped under the name of Amun-Re.

Amenemhet I transferred the capital from Thebes back to Memphis which was much more strategically located. In its neighborhood he built a new residential palace to which he gave the proud name of *Ichtawy,* which may be translated, "he who holds the two lands." The kings of the Twelfth Dynasty restored the custom of building their tombs in the form of pyramids, which are very modest compared to those of the Old Kingdom. They are made entirely of brick with a thin revetment of stone which today has practically disappeared. While the first rulers built their pyramids near Memphis, *Sesostris* II (1897-1879 B.C.) and *Amenemhet* III (1840-1792 B.C.) had theirs erected near the entrance to the Fayum, an oasis to the west of the Nile, which lies by a lake fed by waters of the Nile when it overflows its banks. Sesostris II was the first king to start the colonization of the Fayum in a great scale. The complex of the pyramid and funerary temples of Amenemhet III, in complete ruin today, was still standing in the days of the Ptolemies, and was compared by the Greeks with the Minoan labyrinth of Crete, and considered one of the seven wonders of the world. The mastaba-like tombs of the ladies of the court of Sesostris II discovered in Illahun displayed before the eyes of the excavators the wealth and the high quality of jewelry used in the days of the Twelfth Dynasty.

To house the workers engaged in the building of the pyramid of Illahum a little town was built which was abandoned soon after the rule of Amenemhet III. Covered by the sands of the desert, the town of Kahun was preserved from the ravages of time to be brought to light again by the spade of the archeologists. Since most of what is known of Egyptian life comes from tombs, it is a boon to have from this once prosperous settlement in Kahun a better insight into Egypt's everyday life.

Feudal lords retained considerable power down to the reign of *Sesostris* III, as can be seen from the many imposing rock-tombs they left in Assuan, Beni-Hasan, and elsewhere, and which contrast favorably with the rather modest royal pyramids of this period. But it is also true that the tomb inscriptions evince greater respect for the reigning Pharaoh. On the walls of a tomb in Beni Hasan was found the relief scene which portrays a bedouin caravan of tinkers and instrument players, some of their number riding asses, some walking, as they were entering Egypt. This used to be associated with the story of Joseph and his brothers in Egypt.

But during the course of the reign of Sesostris III (1878-1841 B.C.) the rock tombs of the nomarchs cease unexpectedly. Apparently this monarch ended with a blow the dangerously powerful institution of feudalism. No more nomarchs in the former sense are known either from the late Middle Kingdom period or from the New Kingdom.

In summary we may say that the three important tasks before the kings of the Middle Kingdom were: the consolidation of the state after the chaos of the First Intermediate Period, the colonization of the Fayum, and the annihilation of feudalism. With the exception of the submission of Lower Nubia completed under Sesostris III, there were no wars of conquest of foreign lands worth mentioning. Nubia was at that time, and as late as the New Kingdom, a source of gold. The possession of the Nubian valley was assured by the erection of several fortresses at strategic points. Likewise the route of access from Koptos to the Red Sea through the Wadi Hammamat was made sure by military force. This route was a vital line of communication with the Sinai Peninsula where copper and turquoise were mined, as well as with the land of Punt farther south on the Red Sea. Punt is believed to be modern Somaliland, and was the source of incense and spices.

Contacts with Palestine and Syria by land were made by a road skirting the Mediterranean coast. Some idea of living conditions in neighboring Asia can be gathered from the story of Sinuhe referred to above. Of the military campaigns to Palestine all that is known comes from the stela of an officer found in Abydos which mentions a campaign of Sesostris III to Shechem in central Palestine. But an occupation of Palestine during the Middle Kingdom is out of the question. Commercial relations with Byblos and Crete were carried on. Cretan pottery of the Middle Minoan II period has been found in Egypt together with wares of the Middle Kingdom. Some trade contacts must have been made even with Mesopotamia, since in a find from the time of *Amenemhet* II (1929-1898 B.C.) were associated Mesopotamian wares identified by the style to belong to the Ur III period.

11
SECOND INTERMEDIATE PERIOD

We follow in this survey those historians who reckon the Thirteenth and Fourteenth Dynasties as belonging to the Second Intermediate Period. The division is admittedly arbitrary since there is no sharp break in culture, but only a gradual deterioration of the royal power during these two dynasties, paving the way to the conquest of Egypt by the Hyksos. According to the best chronology, the Thirteenth and the Fourteenth Dynasties cover the period from 1778 to 1670 B.C., while the Fifteenth and Sixteenth Dynasties, the so-called Hyksos Dynasties, cover the period from 1670 to 1570 B.C.

Most kings of the Thirteenth Dynasty carry the name of *Sebekhotep*, which means, "the crocodile-god is pleased." These kings were worshipers of Sebek whose sanctuary was at Gebelen, slightly south of Thebes. This group of kings ruled over all of Egypt. Several of their statues are known, some of colossal proportions, and in the form of a sphinx. But their artistic quality is evidently much inferior to the high artistic level prevailing during the Twelfth Dynasty. According to the historian Stock, after a period of confusion at the end of the Twelfth Dynasty, the Sebekhoteps took over and reigned down to 1710 B.C.

Manetho's Fourteenth Dynasty would have reigned in Xois in the western part of the Delta. The damp condition of the soil in this region would explain why practically no traces have been found of this dynasty. At any rate it never ruled over all of Egypt, and must be regarded as unimportant historically.

The Hyksos
The penetration of the Hurrians into northern Mesopotamia during the first half of the second millennium seems to have set into motion older populations which occupied Syria

and Palestine. Under pressure from the north a segment of this population would have entered Egypt first peacefully, and later in full force, with the help of superior war equipment including the horse-drawn chariot. To these invaders, composed of a Semitic stratum mixed with Hurrian and Aryan elements which dominated Lower Egypt during a century, historians give the name of Hyksos. The Hurrian character of the name of Khian, one of the Hyksos rulers, has not been proved to the satisfaction of all. But the Hurrian name of a slave has been identified on an ostrakon of the Eighteenth Dynasty, and the Hurrian-Aryan term for "chariot-fighter" or "noble," namely *marianni* was adopted into Egyptian.

The designation Hyksos comes from an Egyptian word which means "rulers of foreign lands." Much later Manetho applied it to the Asiatics who dominated Egypt during the last part of Second Intermediate Period. But Manetho missed the meaning when he translated Hyksos as "shepherd kings."

It is customary to call the Fifteenth Dynasty the period of the "great Hyksos" and the Sixteenth that of the "small Hyksos." Of most of these kings only the name is known. Their capital being at Avaris in the damp eastern Delta, very few archeological remains survived. Some kings have good Egyptian names like *Apophis* (Apepi); others have Semitic names like *Jacob-her* or *Anat-her*. The name of the most powerful of them all, *Khian,* is linguistically an enigma. The lid of a diorite vase found in the Palace of Knossos in Crete carries his name, as well as a small basalt lion which came to light in Bagdad. But such finds prove nothing concerning the extent of the Hyksos empire, as formerly believed. Inscriptions of the Hyksos kings have been found even in Gebelen in Upper Egypt, and scarabs of these two dynasties have come to light as far south as Kerma in the Sudan without proving that the Sudan was under their rulership.

The location of their capital Avaris, formerly disputed, has been identified by the French archeologist Pierre Montet with that of the city of Ramesses of the Nineteenth Dynasty, later called Tanis (Biblical Zoan). Great fortifications of beaten earth (*terre pisée*), usually rectangular in plan, such as found in Shechem, Lachish, Tell Beit Mirsim, etc. all from the Middle Bronze Age, have been ascribed to the Hyksos, who are believed to have occupied Palestine at the same time that they controlled Egypt. But no such fortifications have been found in Egypt. Sir Flinders Petrie thought he had found one in Tell

Judeideh in the Delta, but later excavations proved it to be the remains of an Egyptian temple.

The Hyksos are credited with the introduction of the horse and chariot into Egypt. It is supposed that precisely the horse and the war-chariot gave them a decided advantage over the Egyptians in the war of conquest. In Egyptian representations the horse appears for the first time in the tomb painting of the early Eighteenth Dynasty, therefore soon after the period of the Hyksos. Besides the Egyptian word for horse is *ssm.t* clearly related to the Indo-Aryan *sisu*. Only after the Egyptians themselves adopted the horse and chariot in their warfare were they able to expel the hated foreigners. Equally important for Egyptian supremacy was the adoption of the powerful composite bow, and the establishment of a permanent army in which Nubian mercenaries figure prominently.

Circumstantial evidence points to the period of the Hyksos as the most likely for the sojourn of Joseph and the Israelites in Egypt. As Asiatics they would be welcomed by fellow Asiatics. Their abode in a fertile region near the capital of Avaris on the eastern Delta also favors this view. No inscription, though, referring to their permanence in Egypt has yet been found.

The hatred against the Hyksos which is evident in the literature of the early New Kingdom found its main supporters in a ruling family of Thebes, which history counts as the Seventeenth Dynasty. With the war leading to the expulsion of the Hyksos the New Kingdom begins.

12

THE NEW KINGDOM

I. Rise of Egypt to a World Power (*c.* 1610-1413 B.C.)

The initiative to free Egypt from the rule of the Hyksos belongs to a princely family from Thebes which is reckoned as the Seventeenth Dynasty. These Theban kings must at first have ruled as vassals of the Hyksos over their own nome. But with *Sekenenre* I the war of liberation probably began. *Sekenenre* III apparently died of head injuries in battle. His mummy was found by Maspero in a cache in the mountains near the temple of Der el-Bahari among the mummies of many other kings from the Seventeenth to the Twentieth Dynasty. Alarmed by the report of a commission that many royal tombs had been robbed, a king of the Twenty-first Dynasty had the sarcophagi hid to protect the royal mummies from further desecration. The sarcophagi of the Seventeenth Dynasty are recognized by the fact that they have painted on them the figure of the dead in a feathery garment. With the New Kingdom begins the custom of fashioning the coffin in the shape of a mummy.

Concerning the expulsion of the Hyksos there are two literary documents extant. One is a papyrus from the reign of Merenptah which relates that the Hyksos ruler Apophis once sent to king Sekenenre in Thebes a message complaining that the noise made by the hippopotami in the southern capital four hundred miles away did not let him sleep in his palace in Avaris. It sounds like Apophis was trying to pick a pretext for a quarrel. Sekenenre replied in a conciliatory tone, thus showing that he was not yet ready to start war against the Hyksos. But the fact that his mummy shows severe head wounds is taken as evidence that he was soon involved in war against the invaders. The other is a wood-tablet from a student which contains what very likely is the copy of a lost memorial inscription. [1] This mentions how

---

1. Pritchard, *Ancient Near Eastern Texts*, p. 232.

king *Kamose* asked for the advice of his counselors in face of
dangers which threatened Egypt both from Nubia in the south
and from the Hyksos in the north. In spite of their contempor-
izing advice he carried on with vigor the war of liberation.
Kamose recovered all of Egypt from Apophis III except for his
capital Avaris.

The one to complete the liberation of Egypt from the Hyksos
was king *Amosis,* probably a younger brother of Kamose, and
who appears in the kings' list as the founder of the Eighteenth
Dynasty. The Egyptian equivalent to Amosis is Yahmes, which
means, "the moon is born." A very common name in the
Eighteenth Dynasty is Thutmosis, "born of Thot," where Thot
is also the name of the moon-god. This shows the popularity
of the moon-god in this period. King Amosis would have ruled
from 1567 to 1545 B.C., if the Sothis date given by the Ebers
Papyrus for the ninth year of his son and successor *Amenophis* I
is reckoned from Memphis.

The tomb inscriptions of an officer of king Amosis, found in
el-Kab in Upper Egypt, depicts very graphically the conquest
of Avaris and shows that at first the Hyksos were pursued only
as far as Sharuhen in southern Palestine, which was conquered
after a three-year siege. The internal consolidation of Egypt
seems to have been achieved without difficulty. Only in Lower
Nubia had Amosis to fight in order to crush a revolt against
Egyptian domination.

The successor of king Amosis was *Amenophis* I, the first of
four kings of the Eighteenth Dynasty which carry the Egyptian
name Amenhotep "Amun is pleased." If the Sothis date from
his ninth year is correctly interpreted, Amenophis I would have
ruled from 1545 to 1524 B.C. Little is actually known of his
reign, but he must have made a deep impression upon his contemporaries and their descendants, since his name was given
to a yearly feast, and still later it became the name of a month
in Coptic.

He was succeeded by *Thutmosis* I who appears to have been
Amenophis' son-in-law. He was the first to carry the conquest
of Nubia as far as the fourth cataract. To commemorate this
exploit he erected a victory stela in front of the island of
Tombos. Nubia became an Egyptian province, and its administration was placed in the hands of "the king's son of Kush"
whose seat of office was in el-Kab in Upper Egypt. Thutmosis
I then led an expedition to Palestine and Syria as a preventive
military operation against any future threat from Asia, crossing

in the undertaking the Euphrates, on the eastern bank of which
he erected a victory stela. He was also the first pharaoh of the
Eighteenth Dynasty to resume work in the great temple of
Amun in Thebes. He left two obelisks which flanked the entrance to the temple. Thutmosis I ended, once for all, with the
custom of burying kings under a pyramid. As his burial place
he selected a rock tomb in the Valley of the kings to the west
of Thebes, his example being followed by all the kings down
to the Twentieth Dynasty. The remarkable achievements of
this great king were only exceeded by those of his son and second successor *Thutmosis* III.

Thutmosis II, who must have reigned only a few years, was
the son of Thutmosis I through a concubine. According to
some investigators his mummy shows the traces of a sickly young
man, but this verdict has not received the unanimous support
of anatomists. That his reign must have been very brief is
evinced by the almost absolute absence of monuments or inscriptions from his reign.

He was followed by the famous royal pair Queen *Hatshepsut*
and *Thutmosis* III. Hatshepsut was the daughter of Thutmosis I
with Queen Ahmose of royal blood. As such, Hatshepsut was
regarded by a party in the court as the only legitimate heir
to the throne. To legitimize his position Thutmosis II seems to
have married his half-sister. Later Thutmosis III did the same,
since he, too, was the son of a marriage of second rank. But
Hatshepsut who apparently was older than her brother-husband
relegated him to the position of prince-consort, and during
twenty years ruled Egypt as the legitimate pharaoh. The autobiography of Enene found in his tomb in Thebes says expressly,
"When Thutmosis II went to heaven his son took his place as
king of the two lands and ruled on the throne of his father. His
sister, Queen Hatshepsut, cared for the land and led it; Egypt
was submissive to her, to the royal seed; her rule was distinguished, and she made both lands happy with her utterance."
In this inscription Thutmosis III is called son of Thutmosis II,
but this is better interpreted as a matter of protocol.

As pharaoh, Hatshepsut assumed her own throne-name *Ma-
kare,* "truth is the soul of Re." The numerous statues of
Hatshepsut which have survived represent her as a man, and
with the customary crowns and emblems of the male pharaoh;
in the inscriptions of the magnificent temple of Der el-Bahari,
built by her command, she is always referred to by the third
masculine pronoun. Her prime-minister was Senmut who made

Mortuary temple of Queen Hatshepsut at Der el-Bahari in western Thebes.
Courtesy, S. H. Horn

himself immortal by the construction of the terrace-temple of
Der el-Bahari, which lies on the northern end of the Theban
necropolis. The sanctuary itself lies on the third terrace partly
encased in the mountain side. The colonnade halls of the lower
terraces bear rich relief scenes. One of these represents a famous
expedition to the land of Punt usually identified with Somaliland. One may see how the incense trees were loaded on the
Egyptian boats which had sailed down the coast of the Red Sea,
and how these trees were finally planted before the temple of
Der el-Bahari. Another relief presents the royal couple of Punt
greeting the Egyptian expedition, the queen being depicted as
a negress.

The rule of Queen Hatshepsut apparently came to a tragic
end. The prince-consort Thutmosis III, with the support of
the army, must have at last asserted his authority. Evidences of
violence are visible in the partial destruction of the relief scenes
in the temple of Der el-Bahari, the shattering of many of the
statues of the queen, and in the destruction of the tomb of her
vizier Senmut, who disappeared without leaving a trace. Even
the mummy of Queen Hatshepsut apparently fell prey to the
destructive rage of Thutmosis III frustrated in his ambition
for so many years.

His independent rule must have begun c. 1480 B.C. and
lasted till 1448 B.C. In his first year he led a military expedition to Palestine and conquered Megiddo. His forces then
turned against a coalition of Palestinian and Syrian rulers
headed by the king of Kadesh on the Orontes. A detailed report of this expedition was engraved on the walls of the temple
in Karnak. Historians wished reports of the other fifteen expeditions had been recorded with the same detail. The object
of all these campaigns was the subjugation of the numerous
North Syrian states, and the contention of the powerful kingdom of Mitanni on the northern Euphrates. Kadesh was taken
in the sixth expedition but quickly recovered from the blow,
and prepared itself to defy Egyptian sovereignty once more. In
the eighth expedition the river Euphrates was crossed, the land
of Mitanni devastated but only a small number of the enemy
captured. The king then erected a stela on the eastern bank of
the Euphrates near that of his father Thutmosis I. Next he directed his attention once more to the indomitable city of Kadesh.
As the line of battle was drawn under the walls of the city, the
prince of Kadesh resorted to the clever ruse of releasing a mare
before the array of Egyptian chariots each of which was drawn

by a pair of stallions. Only the brave intervention of general Amenemhab saved the Egyptian chariotry from falling into utter confusion. He jumped from his chariot, rushed to the front and killed the mare with a blow of his sword. Commissioned by the king to storm the city, Amenemhab invested against the wall with a few picked troops, and was the first to enter the doomed city through a breach. From the number of dead and captives reported it is clear that the armies involved in these expeditions were rather small.

Tombs of army officers of this time contain the description of personal bravery in these wars, as the one of Amenemhab reported above, and the wall paintings give an idea of the riches which found their way to the royal palace as tributes of war or presents. These paintings more often portray Syrians which are easily distinguished from the Egyptians by their garb, their beard and the fact that they are usually stouter. One relief shows Kefti warriors from Crete, and one a Hittite. Contact with the Hittites became more numerous in the following century as both powers vied for the control of northern Syria. As a result of all these campaigns Egypt achieved complete control of the Mediterranean coast as far north as the mouth of the Orontes river, while assuring at the same time access to the Euphrates. In the list of countries paying tribute to Egypt to be seen in the Annal Halls of the temple of Karnak figures the land of Cheta (Hittites), Assyria, Babylon, Cyprus, and Mitanni. Later friendly relations were established with the last named country, so much so that Mitannian princesses appear in the harem of the pharaoh.

The empire founded by Thutmosis III stretched for two thousand miles from the mouth of the Orontes in the north to the Nubian city of Napata in the south. This intelligent monarch tried to bind the subjugated princes in a friendly relation with Egypt by educating their children in the court at Thebes. The last twelve years of his rule Thutmosis III devoted to the organization of the empire, and to building activities especially in the main sanctuary of Amun in Karnak. The immense treasures which flowed to this temple were administered by a high priest, whose power was only inferior to that of the king. During this dynasty the high-priest of Amun in effect acted as a sort of finance minister.

At the head of the civil administration there were two viziers, one for Upper and one for Lower Egypt. They were directly appointed by the king. No codified law comparable to the Law Code of Hammurabi is known from Egypt. But courts of justice were known from the earliest times. There is a perceptible tendency for military officers to rise in the social scale as result of the wars of Thutmosis III. Above the priesthood and the civil and military administration, stood the pharaoh as absolute ruler, revered as the son of the god Amun-Re. The contrasting position of the king in the Old Kingdom and the New Kingdom is compared by Edward Meyer to that of the enlightened despotism of Louis XIV in France and that of Charlemagne respectively. In both cases about a thousand years separate them.

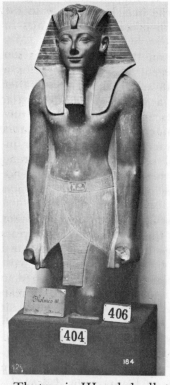

Thutmosis III from Karnak in the Cairo Museum.
Courtesy, S. H. Horn

Thutmosis III ruled all together fifty-four years, of which twenty-two were as prince-consort with Hatshepsut, and thirty-two in his own right. In the thirtieth year of his appointment as heir to the throne he was able to celebrate the thirty-year jubilee commemoration, known as the *heb-sed* festival. Since this festivity was repeated every three or four years after the first celebration, he enjoyed several more jubilees in the next two decades of his reign. It was customary to erect an obelisk for every such celebration, but none of the four obelisks erected in his honor stand any longer in their original place. Today one is found in Constantinople, another in Rome, another in London, and the fourth constitutes a landmark in Central Park in New York.

The mummy of this king was laid to rest in a magnificent tomb in the Valley of the Kings. Robbers eventually broke into the tomb, looted it, and even broke the stone sarcophagus, hacking the mummy into three pieces. Here it was found by guards of the necropolis, carefully rewrapped in the original binding, and transferred to the cache in a lonely place in the mountains where it was found with other royal mummies in 1881.

The successor of Thutmosis III on the throne was his son *Amenophis* II who had been coregent with his father for a short while. He ruled between 1448 and 1422 B.C. Soon after assuming power he had to crush a revolt in Palestine-Syria. He also advanced to the Euphrates and consolidated the conquests made by his father. An inscription found in Nubia speaks of his cruel treatment of war prisoners. In another inscription he boasts of his physical prowess, claiming that no one in his army was able to bend his bow. From the evidence it seems right to conclude that the remainder of his rule was a peaceful one.

The same is true of the rule of his son and successor *Thutmosis* IV, who remained on the throne only nine years (1422-1413 B.C.), dying at the age of thirty. His best-known monument is the great stela which he erected between the paws of the great sphynx. On this he relates how a god appeared to him in a dream and told him to remove the sand that threatened to submerge the sphynx. It is apparent that in his days it had already been forgotten that the sphynx had been built by order of pharaoh Chefren of the Fifth Dynasty. He is the last king of the Eighteenth Dynasty to have campaigned personally in Syria. One of his wives was a princess from the kingdom of Mitanni who became the mother of his successor *Amenophis* III.

II.　Egypt in the Enjoyment of World-Power

The rule of *Amenophis* III (1413-1377 B.C.) represents the high-point of the New Kingdom. His was a long and peaceful reign of thirty-six years, during which he reaped leisurely what his predecessors sowed in their laborious campaigns in Asia and Nubia. He led only one campaign in Nubia in the fifth year of his rule, and it is highly unlikely that he ever set his foot in Asia even though flattering officials made sure that on the monuments his fictitious military exploits were commemorated. There is more truth to the inscription on a scarab that his majesty killed 102 lions in the first ten years of his rule.

To celebrate his wedding with Tiy, the daughter of a commoner, Amenophis III ordered exceptionally large scarabs to be made which were distributed throughout the country. In these scarabs Queen Tiy is expressly called the first wife of the king, in spite of her lowly origin. She seems to have possessed an exceptionally strong personality, and to have exerted a great influence upon the king. In her honor the pharaoh had a great lake excavated not far from the palace on the western bank of Thebes in just fourteen days, and this gave occasion to a new edition of commemorative scarabs. Other scarabs were issued to celebrate some of the king's hunting expeditions, or his marriage to some Mitannian princess.

Like Djoser of the Third Dynasty, Amenophis III was favored with the administrative talent of a highly gifted individual, Amenhotep by name. From the rank of the scribes Amenhotep rose to become chief scribe and chief architect of the realm, besides bearing some military commands. In his tomb inscription he tells how he supervised the quarrying of a large statue of the king, and how he had it erected in one of the courts of the temple of Karnak. How many other works of art can be ascribed to him is not known, but he was regarded as one of the sages of Egypt, and sayings of his were still current in the time of the Ptolemies.

Amenophis III built lavishly, the most ambitious of his undertakings being the temple of Luxor devoted to Amun, situated not far to the south of the temple of Karnak. This colonnade temple was built right on the bank of the Nile, and gives the impression of a gigantic forest of stone. Of his mortuary temple built south of Medinet Habu nothing remains except two colossal statues of the king in a seated position, which the Greeks named, "the colossi of Memnon." They rise seventy feet high in the open country by the Nile.

Of Egyptian influence on world politics much information may be gathered from the Amarna Letters found by a poor peasant woman in a mound in Middle Egypt in 1887. These consist of more than three hundred tablets written in cuneiform, the best translation of which is found in Knudtzon's *Die Amarna Tafeln*. These tablets came from the royal archives of Amenophis III and IV, and show clearly how Egyptian prestige in Palestine and Syria was decaying fast. Some tablets are letters from the kings of Babylon and Mitanni requesting the pharaoh to send them some gold since they have heard there is plenty of it in Egypt. The majority are requests from local kinglets in Palestine or Egyptian officers for troops to be dispatched against the Khapiru which were raiding the country.

Egypt's position as a world empire must have had no small effect on the religious thinking of the time. If the magnificent pharaoh ruled over Syria and Nubia then the gods of Egypt, or at least the sun-god, must exert a comparable sovereignty. From this to the idea of a universal god was only a step. Thus we find under the next pharaoh the solar disc being worshiped as the only universal god.

Columns of the great temple at Luxor in Upper Egypt.
Courtesy, S. H. Horn

13

THE AMARNA PERIOD

Amenophis IV (1377-1358 B.C.) was the son of Amenophis III and Queen Tiy. The religious trend towards a sort of monotheism barely perceptible during the reign of his father now comes to the forefront. Probably encouraged by the sun-priests of Hermonthis, the Heliopolis of Upper Egypt, Amenophis IV soon after inheriting the throne embarked on a religious reform which aimed at nothing less than replacing the worship of Amun or any other god by that of Aten, conceived as the solar disk, the source of all blessings. A sort of syncretism had been going on in Hermonthis whereby the sun-god Re-Harakhti "Re-Horus of the horizon" was identified with Aten and then also with Shu, another solar deity.

Hampered in his efforts to foster the worship of Aten by the priests of Amun at Thebes, the king in his sixth year moved the capital to Amarna, located halfway between the two ancient cities of Thebes and Memphis. The grandiose plans for the new capital never reached completion, since they were abandoned soon after the death of the king twelve years later. Contrary to ancient tradition, the cemetery of Akhetaten, "the horizon of Aten," as the new city was named, was located not on the border of the western desert, but to the east. This choice was influenced by the new religion in which the worship of Aten at sunrise must have had special significance. As before the tombs are carved in the mountain sides, but the relief scenes in them belong to a completely different style. Old artistic canons are laid aside and the scenes are represented true to life. As a result some of the most exquisite paintings of scenes in nature date from this period, as for example that of a cat prowling through the reeds in a marsh. The monarch is often shown together with his wife and children, or with his mother. In these portraits Akhenaten presents an effeminate appearance but not unlike that of his father Amenophis III. On the wall of the tomb of the courtier Eye, who is depicted in a praying position with his wife, was found the often-quoted hymn to Aten which describes in touching terms the divine care for all creation. It has been many times compared with Psalm 104.

In his reformatory zeal Amenophis IV not only changed his theophoric name to that of Akhenaten, "He who is Beneficial to Aten," but did his best to erase the name of Amun from all monuments and inscriptions, even from the names of his father and of his ancestor Amenophis II. If Akhenaten had any hope that great numbers of Egyptians would adopt the new religion he was bound to be disappointed. His exalted monotheistic faith was too advanced for his age. The average Egyptian was an eclectic by temperament who sensed no contradiction in the different theologies of Memphis or Heliopolis, rather regarded them all as complementary explanations of the ultimate reality. Akhenaten's insistence on a single sweeping generalization to explain the many-sided aspects of nature, no matter how convincing, was bound to offend age-old prejudices among the masses.

If few shared Akhenaten's devotion to Aten, at least the king found an enthusiastic supporter of the new religion in his wife Nefretete, who is believed to have been a foreign princess. Her bust, which can be seen today in a museum in West-Berlin, is admired as one of the master-pieces of the Amarna Age.

While Akhenaten spent his life preoccupied with religious reform, Egyptian prestige in Asia sank to a low ebb. As the Amarna Letters abundantly show, no effort was made by the court to answer the frantic appeals for help made by some princes who still professed loyalty to Egypt. The most common complaint in these letters is that unless Egypt would send troops urgently the land would fall into the hands of the Khapiru. Some historians are inclined to see in these Khapiru the Hebrews of the Bible who at this time were overrunning Palestine.

After a reign of nineteen years Akhenaten died without leaving a male heir. His burial place is unknown and his mummy has not been identified with any assurance. He was succeeded by his son-in-law *Sakare,* also read Semenkhare, husband of his oldest daughter Meritaten "Beloved of Aten." Steindorff, among others, thinks that Semenkhare became co-regent for three years with his father-in-law, but died before Akhenaten himself.[1]

1. G. Steindorff and K. C. Seele, *When Egypt Ruled The East,* p. 222f.

Sakare disappears from history after a short reign, and is replaced by *Tutenkhaten* who had married *Ankhesenpaten,* the third daughter of Akhenaten. Under him a violent reaction set in against the worship of Aten. The king changed his name to Tutenkhamun, and the royal court returned to Thebes. The capital Akhetaten, after a brief occupation of twelve years, was definitely abandoned, soon to be covered by the sands of the desert. The accidental discovery of the Amarna tablets led to systematic excavations which unearthed the ruins of the ancient capital. A reconciliation was made between the court and the priests of Amun who regained the ascendancy. The name of Aten was erased from the monuments, and Akhenaten's memory was cursed as that of a heretic.

Little would be said about Tutenkhamun's brief reign, were it not for the fact that his funerary chamber was discovered intact by Howard Carter in 1922. The immense wealth deposited in his tomb and which escaped the cupidity of robbers reflects the gratitude of the priests of Amun for his role in restoring the old religion. His mummy shows that he must

Sarcophagus of Tutekhamun in tomb at Thebes.
Courtesy, S. H. Horn

have died at the age of twenty, and if nine years of reign are allowed to him, then he must have come to the throne as a child of eleven. This would make him a docile tool in the hands of the priests of Amun. Much of the decorative art in the tomb of Tutenkhamun is clearly in the style of the Amarna Age.

The young monarch was succeeded by *Eye,* who had been a high-official in the court of Amarna. It is not clear how he happened to come to the throne not being of royal lineage. His wife Tiy had been the nurse of Akhenaten. He calls himself regularly the "God's Father," which might indicate some relationship to the royal house not clear to us today. Some think he may have married the widow of Tutenkhamun to legitimize his position, but this is not born out by inscriptions in his tomb in Thebes which refer to Tiy as his wife. Already an old man, Eye reigned only five years (1349-1345 B. C.). His tomb was found in the Valley of the Kings close to that of Amenophis III. With him the Eighteenth Dynasty ran out its course.

The Amarna Age has been variously appraised by different historians. While some acclaim it as one of the brilliant periods in the history of religion and art in Egypt, others are inclined to censure Akhenaten· and his immediate successors for their negligence of Egyptian international prestige. The indifference of Akhenaten to the appeal for help contained in the Amarna Letters may be due to the fact that he did not feel right to subjugate foreign nations to Egyptian domination, nor to risk the life of his subjects on foreign adventures. On the other hand it is conceivable that the pharaohs simply did not want to involve themselves in the petty squabbles between the different states of Palestine and Syria, which is the main theme of the letters addressed to the Egyptian court. Akhenaten himself, like all strong personalities, has been variously judged by different schools of thought. To some he was no more than a short-sighted fanatic or an intolerant visionary. To others he was "the first individual in history," the first who dared to think for himself, breaking with all bonds of tradition. All must admire his courage to stand alone for what he thought was true.

14

EGYPT UNDER THE NINETEENTH AND TWENTIETH DYNASTIES

Eye was succeeded by general *Haremhab* who in the days of Tutenkhamun had risen to the position of administrator of Egypt and commander of the army. One inscription speaks of his fifty-ninth year of reign. This would be unbelievable in face of the fact that he came to the throne already a mature man. The explanation to the riddle is very likely to be found in the fact that he simply ignored the kings of the Amarna period and posed as the immediate successor of Amenophis III. Such being the case his actual reign would cover the period from 1345 to 1318 B.C. In his zeal for Amun he destroyed the temple of Aten in Thebes, and used part of the material to build two pylons in the temple of Karnak. As further expression of his hatred against the Amarna kings, he erased the name of Eye from all the monuments, and wrote his own name over that of Tutenkhamun. For his funerary temple he appropriated the one of Eye and expanded it.

Haremhab did much to improve the royal administration. He imposed severe penalties on extortioners of the poor. He also took steps to prevent judges from being corrupted by bribes. His legal enactments may be read on one of the pylons at Karnak. The following sentence translated from one of his inscriptions well expresses his political philosophy, "Behold, his majesty spent the whole time seeking the welfare of Egypt." He was buried in a particularly beautiful tomb in the Valley of the Kings in an alabaster sarcophagus.

Even though considered the founder of the Nineteenth Dynasty, Haremhab was not succeeded by his son, but by another general *Ramesses* I. This name which means "Begotten of Re" is the most common among kings of the Twentieth Dynasty,

and points to the renewed popularity of the sun-god Re. That
again a general ascended to the throne shows the increasing
importance of the army as a political force. Counting on a longer
duration of his reign, Ramesses I began work in the Hypostyle
Hall in the Temple of Karnak later completed by his grandson Ramesses II, and also in the great temple of Abydos which
his son Seti I carried to completion. In his second year he
associated as co-regent with himself his son Seti I, and died
soon thereafter.

In the name of *Seti* I is reflected the ascendancy of the god
Seth who, according to Junker, was worshiped in a sanctuary
near Avaris, which dated back to the days of the Old Kingdom.
In fact it is believed that the Ramessides were originally from
the eastern Delta, which became the center of gravity of the
new dynasty. Thebes ceases as political capital, and from now
on remains only the immensely rich religious center of the cult
of Amun.

From his very first year Seti I undertook the restoration of
Egyptian sovereignty in Asia which had been begun by Haremhab. The army appears reorganized in four divisions, each one
known by the name of a deity and fighting as a unit. To the
infantry were attached groups of war chariots, the presence of
which decided many battles of the Ramesside period. With Seti
I begins the custom of depicting the military campaigns on
the north wall of the temple of Karnak. These relief-scenes
show for the first time a complete sequence of events from the
time the expedition left Egypt to its return. But they do not
compare in objectivity with the annal reports of Thutmosis III.
Here for the first time is the word Canaan mentioned in an
Egyptian source. The relief-scene commemorating the victorious
completion of Seti's first campaign in Palestine shows the king
in colossal proportions riding a six-spoked war chariot pulled
by two stallions. Four groups of prisoners of war are shown,
the rope tied to the necks of three prisoners being held in the
hands of the king himself. These very likely represent captive
princes. The fact that most of the prisoners are bearded shows
that they were Semites. Historians occasionally get some help
from stelae like the one erected by Seti I in Bethshan.

As a result of his expeditions Seti I was able to reduce the
greater part of the Palestinian coast to submission. But during
the Nineteenth Dynasty it was no longer possible for Egyptian
troops to reach the Euphrates, neither could they regain control over northern Syria where the Hittites were firmly en-

trenched. In his second year Seti I fought against the Libyans in the western Delta, and carried another raid into northern Palestine meeting some outposts of the Hittites.

Of the building activities of Seti I should be mentioned the erection of the temple of Abydos dedicated to the deities of the circle of Osiris, king of the dead. It is one of the best preserved temples in Egypt, and still enchants the visitor with the fineness of the relief scenes. His tomb in the Valley of the Kings is one of the largest, and particularly impressive is its hall supported by columns, the roof of which is painted blue punctuated with stars. The precious alabaster sarcophagus of the king is one of the treasures of the British Museum.

Seti I was succeeded by his son *Ramesses* II, whose long reign of sixty-seven years represents the last high-point in Egyptian history. With the support of synchronisms from the chronology of neighboring countries in Asia, his reign can be fixed between 1301 and 1234 B.C. Ramesses' II first task was to secure the boundaries of the empire in Palestine and Syria. In his first expedition he crossed the river Kelb not far north of modern Beirut, where he erected a monumental stela. The main threat to Egyptian supremacy in northern Syria was the Hittite king Muwatallis who headed a formidable coalition. Ramesses II led a second expedition in his fifth year, the main purpose of which was to conquer Kadesh on the Orontes. Near this place his troops ran into an ambush laid by Muwatallis and his allies, and only the personal bravery of Ramesses saved his army from a complete rout. This battle took place in 1296 B.C. In no less than five inscriptions Ramesses celebrated this event as an Egyptian victory, but the modern historian must pronounce it a drawn battle at best. Kadesh was not conquered, and northern Syria remained in Hittite hands. In fact the boundary between the two empires remained at the river Kelb. The war between the two empires lasted with interruptions another fifteen years, and only ended with a peace-treaty celebrated between Ramesses II and Hattusilis III in 1280 B.C. The treaty was engraved on Egyptian temples as a religious document, and has also been identified on a cuneiform tablet in Boghazkoy. The original engraved on a silver plate has not been found. To secure the peace Ramesses married a daughter of Hattusilis, in 1267 B.C., who was elevated to the position of "Great Royal Wife." This event was immortalized on a stela at the entrance of the rock temple of Abu Simbel in Aswan, at the border of Nubia. This marriage together with the peace-treaty of 1280 B.C. stabilized conditions in the Near East until with the invasion of the "Sea-peoples" around 1200 B.C. the Hittite kingdom collapsed and Egypt was faced with new invaders.

The accumulated wealth of Egypt resulting from foreign tributes and internal prosperity allowed Ramesses II to indulge in a grandiose building program not equaled by any other pharaoh. In the extreme south he built the temple of Abu Simbel, now threatened with submersion by the rising waters of the Aswan dam. Carved in the mountain side, the front of this temple displays four colossal statues of the king in a sitting position, each of which is sixty feet high. Crossing the great portal one enters into a majestic hall in which two rows of four pillars seem to support the ceiling. In front of each pillar there is a figure of the pharaoh more than thirty feet in height. On the inner walls of the temple, still preserving much of the original color, is to be seen a great representation of the battle of Kadesh.

On the eastern Delta the king rebuilt Avaris as a royal residence, naming it "the city of Ramesses." Its exact location was disputed until the French archeologist Pierre Montet proved its identity with Avaris of the Hyksos period, with Tanis of the Twenty-first Dynasty, and with the Biblical Zoan. Ramesses II also completed the great hypostyle hall of Karnak which had been started by his father Seti I. Its size is large enough to accommodate the whole cathedral of Notre Dame in Paris.

But in spite of the size and number of these constructions, they lag behind those of the Eighteenth Dynasty in artistic quality. One exception to this is the painting found in many tombs of this period, which very often form beautiful and logical composite scenes covering all the walls. These paintings also express a deeper religious feeling than used to prevail in former periods. This more personal religious ethos finds no better expression than in the contemporary "Instructions of Ani," from which we quote: "Do not cry in the dwelling of god; his abomination is clamor. If you have prayed with a loving heart, all your words remaining hidden, he fulfills your need, he hears what you say, he accepts your offering."[1] Another change introduced in this age is the use in the inscriptions of the language actually spoken by the people. The transition from Middle Egyptian to New Egyptian is comparable to the transition from the English of Chaucer to modern English.

---

1. *ANET,* p. 420.

The Israel Stela of Merneptah, the only Egyptian monument mentioning the name of Israel (in white box) in hieroglyphs.

Courtesy, S. H. Horn

Ramesses II died in 1234 B.C. after a long and prosperous rule. For his funerary temple he built the gigantic "Ramesseum" which still stands on the western side of Thebes. His tomb in the Valley of the Kings is rather prosaic. Since he outlived many of his seventy-nine sons, only the thirteenth became his successor on the throne under the name of *Merneptah* (1234-1225).

In his fifth year Merneptah repelled an attack of Libyans and Meshwesh which threatened Egypt from the west. This attack was particularly dangerous because it was related with that movement of peoples known to historians as "Sea-peoples" which set the whole Eastern Mediterranean world in commotion at the end of the thirteenth century B.C. It in turn may have been precipitated by the invasion of the Balkan Peninsula by the Illyrians and Dorians. This mass-migration included the Shirdana (Sardenians), Shakalsha (Sicilians), Tursha (Etruscans), Aqiwasha (Acheans), Luke (Lycians), Peleset (Philistines), and Zakar. These last two peoples seem to have come from Crete. One opinion is that the majority of these peoples came from Asia Minor, and after being repelled from Egypt settled in Sicily, Sardenia, Etrury, etc.

Merneptah celebrated his victory in an inscription at the temple of Karnak, and on a great stela to be seen in the Museum of Cairo. On this he celebrated an expedition to Palestine as well, and on it he mentions for the first and only time in an Egyptian inscription the name of Israel. The stela has been named the "Stela of Israel," and it shows that the Israelites were already occupying at least part of Palestine by the end of the thirteenth century B.C. The poverty which descended upon Egypt after the spending-spree of Ramesses II is clearly seen from the fact that Merneptah used for his memorial the back side of a stela erected by Amenophis III.

According to the best evidence, Seti II followed his father on the throne. Tradition gives him a rule of six years. He was succeeded by *Siptah* whose right to the throne was assured by his marriage to Queen Ta-useret, a daughter of Merneptah. The rivalry between old Thebes and the new capital of Ramesses was exploited by a certain Amenmesses who ruled from Thebes as a rival king for a few years. At least in Thebes he was recognized as king since he was given a tomb in the Valley of the Kings. After the death of Siptah, a usurper, the Palestinian *Irsu,* came to the throne. His rulership is attested by a papyrus, but he left no monuments. Supposedly he reigned in Ramesses for two years until deposed by *Sethnakht* "Seth is strong," the founder of the Twentieth Dynasty.

Sethnakht was a native of Tanis, and possibly related to the old line of Seti I and Ramesses II. His rule was also very short (*c.* 1200-1197 B.C.), but he made sure the ascension of his son *Ramesses* III to the throne. All his successors in this dynasty bore this prestigious name down to Ramesses XI. Ramesses III ruled thirty-two years and may be with right considered the last great king of the New Kingdom. Information concerning his reign comes from several sources: from his well preserved funerary temple in Medinet Habu, from his beautiful tomb in the Valley of the Kings, and also from the longest papyrus preserved from Old Egypt, the Harris Papyrus. The content of this papyrus is an inventory of the treasures of the main Egyptian temples. From this it is evident that the temple of Amun had the lion's share in the royal bequests.

On the outer walls of the temple of Medinet Habu is portrayed the great sea-battle in which Ramesses III beat back the threatened invasion of the Sea-peoples. As the chief enemies of the Egyptians in this battle appear the Peleset and the Zakar. The Philistines are easily recognized by their plumed helmets. After their defeat they settled down on the Palestinian coast south of Dor, where they figure as a dominant group down to the days of David. The Shirdana appear as auxiliary troops on the Egyptian side, showing that the Sea-peoples were willing to engage themselves as mercenary troops to any party willing to hire them. This victory of Ramesses III over the barbarian invaders may be reckoned as one of the great services he rendered Egypt. He also fought victoriously against the Libyans in two campaigns likewise depicted on the walls of the temple of Medinet Habu. Exhausted after these wars, Egypt was not in position to reassert its authority in Palestine. This allowed the Philistines to establish the five city-states of Gaza, Ashkelon, Ashdod, Ekron and Gath, known as the Philistine Pentapolis. At the same time the Israelites were able to consolidate their grip on the hill-country of Palestine without suffering interference from Egypt.

After the death of Ramesses III the kingly power in Egypt underwent a rapid decline. The following eight Ramessides ruled together about eighty years (c. 1165-1085 B.C.). Their capital continued to be the city of Ramesses, and they found their last resting-place as formerly in the Valley of the Kings. Since there was not enough space here for the burial of the many queens and princesses, another valley was chosen much farther south which came to be known as the Valley of the Queens. Except for their tombs, no other monuments are known from these weak Ramessides.

Ramesses XI ruled thirty years, but the end of his rule is shrouded in darkness. Since like his predecessors he ruled from Tanis, it is more likely that he was ousted by *Smendes,* the founder of the Twenty-first Dynasty, who also ruled from Tanis, than by *Herihor* who had established a rival court in Thebes. Herihor, who was the high-priest of the temple of Amun, grounded his claim to power on the only remaining foreign colony of Egypt, namely Nubia, by assuming the old title of "Prince of Cush."

15

PERIOD OF DECADENCE

The Twenty-first Dynasty, (c. 1085 to 950 B.C.) presents the curious anomaly of a double rulership in Egypt, one centered in Tanis, the other in Thebes. Nothing is known of *Smendes* regarded as founder of this dynasty. The picture is not any brighter in Thebes where *Herihor* founded a rival dynasty. What is clear is that his successors in Thebes gradually sank into insignificance. The impression Egypt makes is one of decadence both in military power and in the arts. A picaresque description of the powerless condition of Egypt at the time is to be found in the trip report of Wen-Amun, who undertook a voyage to Byblos in order to procure cedar for the bark of Amun. Everywhere he was mistreated, and people poked fun at the prestige of Egypt which no longer existed. In Dor he was robbed of the little money he carried and was unable to obtain reparations from the authorities. When he arrived in Byblos with his little ship he was told to leave the harbor. He was finally received in audience by the prince who was quite ready to admit the indebtedness of Byblos to the ancient Egyptian civilization, but saw no reason why he should grant the petition of Wen-Amun.

The rulers of this period are all second rank figures. According to prevailing fashion one was called Piankhi "the Living One," another Pinutem "the Sweet." By the marriage of a grandson of Herihor with the daughter of a Tanite king the two houses were brought into better relations, but politically Tanis dominated throughout. Some historians are inclined to believe that Psusenhes, the last pharaoh of this dynasty, was the king who gave his daughter in marriage to king Solomon of Israel.[1]

The political union of Egypt was achieved once more under the Twenty-second Dynasty, known as the Libyan dynasty. It

---

1. I Kings 7:8.

was founded by a family of Libyan military officers who established themselves in Herakleopolis. Entering first as mercenaries in the armies of the Ramessides, they gradually gained in influence and power until *Sheshonk* (Biblical Shishak) ascended to the throne of the pharaohs about 950 B.C. His name is known from Assyrian inscriptions as Shushinqu. The Libyan dynasty ruled from Bubastis, a city on the western Delta, known in the Bible as Pi-beseth.[2] To the Egyptians it was the city of the cat-goddess Bastet. These rulers did away with the priestly dynasty of Thebes, and established the custom that a prince of the ruling house became high-priest of Amun, but without the right of making the post hereditary. Thus Thebes was again firmly bound to the royal house.

As many Libyan mercenaries in the Delta came to prominent positions, which became hereditary, a soldier's caste was formed. Since the position of priest was likewise hereditary gradually a priestly class crystallized. When the Greeks came to know Egypt after the seventh century they got the wrong impression that the caste system had prevailed in the country of the Nile from the very beginning. This impression so often repeated in the literature is obviously incorrect. Innumerous autobiographies found in tomb inscriptions make clear that many high officers in the royal service rose from the ranks, and that native ability and hard work were the chief assets for promotion in public life.

In his fifth year *Sheshonk* I undertook an expedition against Palestine which is reported in I Kings 14. Since this took place in the fifth year of Rehoboam, historians have here an opportunity to correlate the dates of both kings. The expedition turned out to be merely a plundering raid to replenish the empty treasury of Egypt. To commemorate the campaign Sheshonk caused a great historic relief to be engraved on a wall in the temple of Karnak. The inscription mentions one hundred and fifty-three cities many of which have been identified. This is the last historical relief to be engraved on the wall of an Egyptian temple. That Egyptian kings continued to meddle in Palestinian affairs during this dynasty is also evident from the report of the battle of Qarqar (853 B.C.) made by Shalmaneser III, where it is mentioned that a contingent of one thousand Egyptian soldiers took part in the memorable battle. Its diminutive size is evidence that by now Egypt was indeed a "broken reed." Several of the latter kings of this dynasty bore the names of Osorkon or Take-

---

2. Ezekiel 30:17.

lot. None of them attained great prominence. *Osorkon* II seems
to have had friendly relations with Omri or Ahab, since an alabaster vase such as the pharaohs used to present to fellow-rulers
was found by Reisner in Samaria in 1924.

Tombs of kings of the Twenty-first and Twenty-second Dynasties, namely of the Tanite and Bubastide dynasts, were unknown until excavated in 1939-1940 by Pierre Montet in the
ruins of Tanis. No great treasures came to light, but even so some
preciosities were found including, for example, a necklace of
lapis lazuli and gold.

The Twenty-third Dynasty was undoubtedly contemporaneous
with the Twenty-second, and is also reckoned as Libyan. Under
this dynasty are counted *Petubastis, Osorkon* III and IV. As for
"So king of Egypt" on whom Hoshea of Israel relied in his
revolt against Assyria in 725/724 B.C. his identity has not been
definitely established. The most recent suggestion is to read the
Biblical text of II Kings 17:4 with a slight emendation, "to So,
to the king of Egypt[3]." *So* then would be the Hebrew way of
pronouncing *Saʒ* (Greek *Sais*), the capital of a minor principality in the Delta. Towards the end of this dynasty the power
of the pharaoh deteriorates rapidly. While several petty kings
tried to carve for themselves principalities in the Delta, the
region around Thebes was occupied by the Ethiopians.

One of these petty kings was *Tefnakht* of Sais. By 730 B.C. he
began to submit the Delta region, and it looked for a while
as if he might unify all of Egypt. But his plans to extend his
rule over Upper Egypt were shattered when he met defeat at
the hands of the powerful Ethiopian king *Piankhi* who already
controlled southern Egypt from his capital Napata in Nubia.

Tefnakht's son *Bochoris* was, according to Manetho, the only
king of the Twenty-fourth Dynasty. He ruled only six years (*c.*
713-708), and while nothing is known about him from Egyptian
sources, the Greeks praised him as a great law-giver. A remarkable demotic papyrus dated from the time of the Roman em-
peror Augustus narrates the prophecy of a lamb uttered in the
sixth year of Bochoris, in which the imminent invasion of Egypt
and its conquest by the Assyrians are predicted. Bochoris was
defeated by the Ethiopian *Shabako,* first king of the Twenty-fifth
Dynasty, and burned alive.

---

3. Hans Goedicke, "The End of 'So, King of Egypt,' " *BASOR* 171 (1963),
   p. 64 ff.

16

LATE PERIOD: PERSIAN RULE

With the Ethiopian Dynasty begins what historians call the Late Period in Egyptian history. The proud empire of the pharaohs is by now only a shadow of its former glory. It languishes for several decades under Ethiopian and Assyrian domination later to regain part of its ancient prestige under the Twenty-sixth Dynasty. After a century and a half of national independence Egypt is invaded and conquered by Medo-Persia. Persian rule lasted for about two centuries broken only by a short period when native rulers again ascend the throne of the pharaohs. When Alexander the Great crushed the armies of Darius III of Persia he was received in Egypt as a "liberator." However interesting the history of Egypt under the enlightened rule of the Ptolemies, it lies beyond the scope of the present survey.

The Ethiopian Period (715-663 B.C.)

About the year 1000 B.C., still in the course of the Twenty-first Dynasty, Nubia must have shaken the Egyptian yoke, and become an independent kingdom with its capital in Napata near the fourth cataract. In its neighborhood several temples and pyramids were excavated by the American archeologist Reisner. These pyramids are much steeper and lower than those of the Old Kingdom, and they also have their funerary temples decorated in typical barbarian style. On the basis of archeological evidence, Reisner was able to reconstruct the history of Nubia for a thousand years. A new population of darker color apparently moved in around 750 B.C., and its king *Kashta* founded the independent kingdom of Napata at that time. Around 300 B.C. the capital, for unknown reasons, was moved farther south to Moeris. Here it remained until about 400 A.D. when it was destroyed by the kingdom of Axum (Abyssinia).

Kashta as soon as opportunity presented itself conquered and annexed Upper Egypt, including Thebes where the fabulously rich temple of Amun was located. Nubian claim to Thebes and the temple of Amun has been explained on the basis of the fact that the founders of the Nubian kingdom were priests of Amun who had been expelled from Thebes. To assure an intimate connection of the temple with the crown, Kashta persuaded the acting "divine wife" of Amun, a daughter of Osorkon III of the Twenty-third Dynasty, to adopt his own daughter as successor.

Kashta was followed by his son *Piankhi*, who at the head of a powerful army defeated Tefnakht of Sais and conquered all of Egypt. He left a very detailed record of this expedition on the Stela of Piankhi, found in the temple of Amun in Napata but today kept in the Cairo Museum. It is one of the most instructive historical texts from ancient Egypt. According to this stela Piankhi undertook the conquest of Egypt in the twenty-first year of his reign, that is, *c.* 725 B.C. City after city fell before his victorious army until he came before the walls of Memphis. He offered the great metropolis generous terms of capitulation, but the city protected by walls on three sides and by the Nile on the fourth prepared to resist the siege. By stealth he captured all the boats of the enemy and stormed the city from the river side. The ruse was successful and Memphis fell. Tefnakht offered submission and was retained as a vassal under oath. Even though victorious, Piankhi is not counted as the founder of the Twenty-fifth Dynasty.

Only with the successor of Piankhi — it is not clear whether his son or brother — king *Shabako,* who defeated and killed Bochoris of the Twenty-fourth Dynasty in 708 B.C., may we date the beginning of the following dynasty. Under the rule of the Ethiopian kings Thebes became the capital once more. The chronology of the Cushite Dynasty has been reworked by Macadam and Albright on the evidence of inscriptions on a temple built by *Taharqo* at Kawa near the third cataract. The probable sequence was as follows: Shabako began to reign in 708 B.C. *Shabitko* was associated with Shabako as co-regent in 699 B.C., and became sole ruler in 697 B.C. *Taharqo,* born in 709 B.C., was associated with Shabitko in 689 B.C., and became sole ruler in 684 B.C.[1]

If the above reconstruction is correct, then Taharqo could not

---

1. Cf. J. Finegan, *Light From the Ancient Past*, p. 127 Note.

have fought against Sennacherib of Assyria in 701 B.C., when Jerusalem was besieged in the days of Hezekiah. This lends support to the theory that Sennacherib led two invasions against Judah, one in 701 B.C., reported in II Kings 18:13 to 19:8, and the other when Taharqo was already king, that is after 689 or 684 B.C., but still before his own death in 681 B.C. This would be the campaign referred to in II Kings 19:9-37, in which the name of Taharqo (Tirhakah) is mentioned. This two-campaign hypothesis removes several difficulties, and is rendered plausible by the fact that the Biblical account gives the impression that Sennacherib died soon after his defeat, which would not be true if all the events mentioned occurred in 701 B.C.

During the Ethiopian Dynasty Assyria was at the height of its power. Egypt tried to encourage revolt against Assyrian domination among the Palestinian kinglets promising them support. But the prophet Isaiah condemned the reliance of the Jewish rulers on Egyptian support, characterizing Egypt as "the dragon do-nothing."

In 671 B.C. Esarhaddon conquered Egypt reducing it to an Assyrian province during seven years. This victory was commemorated by Esarhaddon on a stela found in Sendjerli in northern Syria. In it the king of Tyre who had been defeated at the same time is represented as the more important of the two kings. The same is celebrated on a monumental inscription by the river Kelb adjacent to that of Ramesses II. Taharqo was able to recover from the blow and forced Ashurbanipal to invade Egypt again in 667 B.C. The annals of Ashurbanipal tell how Taharqo was expelled from Memphis and Thebes, and forced to flee to Ethiopia. He died in 664 B.C. and was succeeded by *Tanutamun,* probably a son of Shabako. An inscription found in Napata tells how Tanutamun was inspired by a dream to reconquer Egypt. He was able to push as far north as Memphis, but the Assyrians reacted under Ashurbanipal and carried their conquest as far south as Thebes which was totally destroyed in 663 B.C. The fall of Thebes had immense repercussions, and is mentioned as a momentous happening in Nahum 3:8ff. In spite of this defeat Tanutamun was able to maintain himself in Upper Egypt a few more years, until he finally withdrew to Napata in Nubia.

The Saite Period

In contrast with the Twenty-fifth Dynasty which had its center of gravity in Thebes, the Twenty-sixth had for its capital

Sais in the Western Delta. Its origin goes back to *Neco* who was
a prince of Sais distinguished by Esarhaddon with the title of
king. Because of a conspiracy with Taharqo against Assyria he
was taken prisoner to Nineveh. He knew how to ingratiate himself with Ashurbanipal who restored him to the throne of Sais.
When he was killed by the Ethiopian Tanutamun, his very energetic son *Psammetichus* sought refuge with the Assyrians, and
after the expulsion of the Ethiopians he returned to Sais. In
recognition for his loyal support of Assyria, he was made king
in Memphis, while the Delta was ruled by minor dynasts.

Psammetichus I (663-610 B.C.) took advantage of the decline
of Assyrian power to make Egypt independent, and to unify it
once more under his rule. Most of the information concerning
the Saite period comes from Herodotus who visited Egypt about
445 B.C., and therefore not too long after the Twenty-sixth
Dynasty had run its course. Another source of information is
the Old Testament where Pharaoh Neco is mentioned as we
shall see. Herodotus, in spite of many omissions, is clear on the
point that the southern boundary of Egypt was again at Elephantine where it stood two thousand years before. The cities
which play the more important role now are no longer Thebes
or even Memphis, but the cities of Sais, Buto, Athribis, Bubastis, all on the Delta enriched with the growing Mediterranean
trade. From the religious standpoint what impressed Herodotus
most was the widespread worship of animals. Whereas formerly
only one animal of each kind was considered sacred, like the
bull Apis in Memphis, now it became fashionable for each nome
to regard all the animals of a certain kind sacred, all cats in one
nome, all dogs in another, etc. Herodotus muses what would
happen if the cat-nome should have a quarrel with the dog-
nome. Animal worship led to the expensive custom of embalming animals for burial, a custom which persisted down to
Roman times.

After a long and peaceful reign Psammetichus I was succeeded by his son *Neco* II (609-593 B.C.). At that time Ashur-
uballit II of Assyria was hard pressed by the Babylonians, who
with the help of the Medes had conquered Nineveh in 612 B.C.
According to the *Babylonian Chronicle*, Neco came with an
army to help Ashur-uballit reconquer Harran in 609 B.C. (II
Kings 23:29 and II Chronicles 35:20). The expedition failed
as far as Harran was concerned, but Neco II was able to conquer all of Palestine and Syria, and to hold the important city
of Carchemish on the Euphrates. It was during this campaign

to the north that Josiah of Judah tried to intercept the forces of Neco at Megiddo and was slain. Four years later, in 605 B.C., Neco was defeated by Nebuchadnezzar of Babylon, and had to abandon Carchemish, Syria and Palestine. After this reversal Neco II confined his attention to Egypt, and conceived the grandiose plan of building a canal from the Nile to the Red Sea through Wadi Tumilat. This project was completed one hundred years later by the Persian king Darius I.

Neco was followed on the throne by *Psammetichus* II (593-588 B.C.) who endeavored to reconquer Lower Nubia, but without success. In his days the Greeks founded the trading colony of Naucratis in the Western Delta. He was succeeded by his son *Apries* (588-570 B.C.), who is called Hophrah in Jeremiah 44:30. He entered into an alliance with Zedekiah of Judah against Nebuchadnezzar, but was unable to forestall the fall of Jerusalem in 586 B.C. Apparently he was more successful in reestablishing Egyptian ascendancy over Tyre, perhaps with the intention of cutting the supply lines of Nebuchadnezzar from the rear. It is worth notice that many years after the fall of Jerusalem, Tyre was still resisting a siege by the Babylonian forces. As a result of a miscarried expedition against Cyrene in Libya, the army revolted and drove Apries from the throne, placing in his stead *Amasis*. This king, also known as Ahmose, enjoyed a long and prosperous reign (569-525 B.C.). He married a daughter of Psammetichus II in order to legitimize his position. Herodotus describes him as friendly to the Greeks. A fragmentary cuneiform inscription refers that Nebuchadnezzar in his thirty-seventh year (568/567 B.C.) marched against Amasis. Nothing is known of the outcome of this expedition. Later in the face of the rising power of Cyrus of Persia Amasis joined in a defensive alliance with Lydia and Babylon in the days of Nabonidus king of Babylon (547 B.C.). He equipped a fleet and made Cyprus an Egyptian province.

Amasis' son, *Psammetichus* III, had a short rule of only six months. He was defeated by Cambyses II at the battle of Pelusium (525 B.C.) in the eastern Delta, and made prisoner. Later as he tried to promote an insurrection against the Persians he was executed. Egypt became a satrapy of the Persian Empire.

The Persian Period

Manetho reckons the Persian kings as the Twenty-seventh Dynasty. The conqueror of Egypt, *Cambyses* did little to please the native population. He once showed his spite of the Egyptian gods by killing the bull Apis. The revenue of the temples, with few exceptions, were curtailed. In the attempt to annex the Ethiopian kingdom of Napata Cambyses failed miserably.

After Cambyses the only Persian king to set foot in Egypt was *Darius* I (521-485 B.C.). Darius changed the oppressive policies of Cambyses, and did his best to promote the prosperity and welfare of Egypt, if for no other reason than to increase the royal revenue. He completed the canal begun by *Neco* II connecting the Nile with the Red Sea. Under his benevolent rule many temples were restored, and he even had a temple built to Amun in the oasis of Kharga. Darius died while preparing to crush a revolt in Egypt fostered by a certain Khabbash who had made himself king in Memphis.

Darius' successor *Xerxes* crushed the Egyptian revolt, and appointed his brother Achaemenes as satrap of Egypt. More serious was the revolt against *Artaxerxes* I led by the Libyan dynast Inaros, who had the support of an Athenian fleet of three hundred ships. The revolt ended with the defeat of the Athenians. Under *Darius* II (423-405 B.C.) Egypt was able to regain its independence from Persia. Manetho divided the kings of this period of Egyptian independence into three dynasties. The only king of the Twenty-eighth Dynasty was king *Amyrtaios* (404-399 B.C.) from Sais. He had the support of Greek mercenaries to stave off Persian encroachment.

The Twenty-ninth Dynasty had its origin in Mendes in the eastern Delta, and may be dated from 398 to 379 B.C. To this dynasty belonged *Nepherites* I, *Hakoris, Psammothis* and *Nepherites* II. The only one to achieve distinction was Hakoris who fought successfully a long war against Persian aggression. His name appears upon some monuments and temple inscriptions.

The last native dynasty was the Thirtieth which stemmed from Sebennytos in the middle Delta. This dynasty comprised three kings which together ruled about forty years. But this short period witnessed the last attempt to relive Egypt's ancient glory. Egyptian art saw its last great flourishing in which the style of the Middle Kingdom was imitated with a great degree of ingenuity. The first of these rulers was *Nectanebos* I who repelled a large Persian fleet and army under the command of Pharnabazus, acting under Artaxerxes II. He was succeeded by *Tachos* who planned an attack on the Persian satrapies of Palestine and Syria in the great style of the kings of the Eighteenth Dynasty. In this enterprise he had the support of the Spartan king Agesilaos. As the expedition was meeting with success, Tachos' brother revolted in Egypt. Agesilaos threw his support to the usurper, and Tacho had to seek refuge with the Persians.

The usurper *Nectanebos* II was able to fend off the Persians for a while, and even build in Sebennytos a temple to Isis whose gigantic ruins draw the attention of the modern tourist. But finally Artaxerxes III (Ochos) invaded Egypt with a great army reducing it again to a Persian satrapy. Egypt remained under Persian domination for ten years, until Alexander the Great entered Egypt as a liberator in 332 B.C., after defeating Darius III in the battles of Granicus and Issus. Under the Ptolemies, the successors of Alexander, Egypt enjoyed three hundred years of relative prosperity, but the history of this period belongs already to the Hellenistic times.

17

THE OLD ASSYRIAN KINGDOM

In previous chapters we referred to the invasion of Egypt by the Assyrian kings Esarhaddon and Ashurbanipal in the seventh century B.C. To understand the dominant role which Assyria played in the Near East in the first half of the first millennium B.C. we must review briefly its rise to the position of a world power.

The beginning of the history of Assyria must be sought early in the third millennium, when people of the Tell-Halaf culture were absorbed by the invading Semites, giving origin to a population which was culturally inferior to that of Babylon, but its superior in energy and military élan. Little is known about this early period. The Assyrian king-list, discovered in 1932 in Khorsabad by an expedition of the University of Chicago, only says that the first seventeen rulers were "kings who lived in tents," therefore no more than sheiks of half-nomadic tribes. The sixteenth in this list was *Ushpia* to whom posterity ascribed the building of the temple of Ashur in Ehursagklalamma. His successor *Abazu* may have been a contemporary of Manishtusu of Akkad. Assyria was at that time incorporated into the empire of Sargon (2350-2150 B.C.), and still later was subservient to the rulers of the Third Dynasty of Ur.

With the fall of the Third Dynasty of Ur about 1950 B.C., Assyria regained partial independence. The first king to distinguish himself in this new period was *Ilushuma,* who in two dedicatory inscriptions glories himself with having built the temple of Ishtar in Ashur, to have erected walls, and significantly to have guaranteed the freedom of the Akkadians of Ur, Nippur, Awal and Kismal. This must be understood not as political independence from the West-Semite rulers of Isin and Larsa, but at least as a reaction of the Akkadians against the foreign yoke.

Of more commercial than political importance was the influence which Assyria exerted over an area of Asia Minor during the first quarter of the second millennium. Much light has been shed on this fact by the discovery of more than three thousand tablets in Kultepe and Alishar in modern Turkey, most of them of a commercial nature. These tablets show that Assyria was strong enough to guarantee the caravan routes connecting it with Asia Minor, as well as to protect the lives of Assyrian merchants established in Cappadocia. These Assyrian merchants might be compared with the *metics* in Greece, resident aliens in whose hands lay the bulk of trade. They lived in the outskirts of the cities under their own law, and were not interfered with as long as Assyria was strong enough to protect them. The trade was mainly in metals and raw materials. The intimate relation between these Assyrian trading posts and the homeland is evinced by the discovery in Asia Minor of two copies of a building inscription in which *Erishu* I, successor of Ilushuma, commemorates the construction of the temple of Ashur. These trading colonies were still flourishing under Erishu's grandson *Sargon* I, when they came to an end about 1770 B.C., at the time the Hittites took over Asia Minor.

Enfeebled by the loss of its foreign trade, and hard pressed by the Hurrians from the north, Assyria fell an easy prey to the energetic ruler of Eshnunna, *Naramsin,* who made himself king. But his son *Erishu* II was in turn displaced by the West-Semite *Shamshi-Adad* I, who at the head of a bedouin tribe conquered Ashur in 1749 B.C.

Shamshi-Adad was the son of Ilukabkabu, leader of a prominent family of Mari. As soon as Shamshi-Adad felt strong enough in his Assyrian realm, he made a raid on Mari, deposed the legitimate king Iahdumlin, and set his son Iasmah-Adad on the throne. Little was known of Shamshi-Adad I until the discovery of the archives of Mari by André Parrot, who started excavations in the site in 1935. He was a contemporary of two other great rulers in Mesopotamia, Rimsin of Larsa and Hammurabi of Babylon. In spite of the pressure put on him by his two rivals to the south, and by the Hurrians on the northwest, Shamshi-Adad distinguished himself as a very capable ruler. He not only defended his own territory, but gave full support to his weak son Iasmah-Adad in Mari, and to his other son Ishme-Dagan in Ekallatum. The Mari tablets show him always busy with the administration of his kingdom, directing the military affairs, proccupied with improving agriculture, commerce and transportation. Private letters give us an insight into the daily cares of the monarch: Iasmah-Adad must return a fugitive slave, provide servants for the royal court, send the grown daughter of Iahdumlin to receive music lessons in the court, dispatch the beautiful chariots from Mari to the New-Year festival in Shubatenlil "the abode of Enlil," etc.

Shamshi-Adad I was succeeded by his son *Ishme-Dagan,* who, in spite of his fine qualities, did not have the energy of his father. He ruled during forty years (1716-c. 1677 B.C.), and the correspondence he carried on with his brother in Mari throws much light upon his busy reign. He had to subdue aggressive nomadic tribes, put down a revolt in Iablia, repel an invasion of the Turukku, a mountain-tribe from the north, fight against the king of Eshnunna, and finally make common cause with Eshnunna against more formidable enemies. But here the correspondence suddenly ends, and the annexation of Assyria into the kingdom of Hammurabi must be deduced from circumstantial evidence. In the prologue to his famous code, Hammurabi expresses pride in his care over Nineveh. Possibly Ishme-Dagan continued to rule as a vassal king.

The king-list of Khorsabad lets Ishme-Dagan be followed by a certain *Ashurdugul,* qualified as "a son of nobody," which simply meant somebody without royal pedigree. Then followed six usurpers all in one year. This is indicative of the chaos which preceded the return of Assyria to a period of obscurity which lasted two hundred years. The absence of documents from this period is interpreted by Gelb as evidence that Assyria was overrun by some barbarian tribe, possibly the Turruku, until the Hurrians themselves took over control of Assyria. [1]

---

1. Ignace Gelb, *Hurrians and Subarians,* p. 66.

18

MIDDLE ASSYRIAN KINGDOM

Of the next two centuries of Assyrian history we know little besides the names of its rulers as furnished by the Khorsabad king-list. By the end of the sixteenth century we read of rulers like *Shamshi-Adad* III and *Ashur-nirari* I who called themselves only "ensi of Ashur." They are very likely under tribute to the Hurrian kings of Mitanni, and only occasionally do we have from them building inscriptions which tell of work in temples, palaces or city-walls.

Some welcome light on this period is cast by the "Synchronistic History," a historical work from the library of Ashurbanipal which deals with the relations between Assyria and Babylon in a synchronistic way. According to this source *Puzur-Ashur* III (*c.* 1490-1470 B.C.) may have had a conflict with the Kassite king of Babylon Karaindash, which was finally settled by a boundary agreement. At the beginning of the fourteenth century Assyria takes advantage of the anarchy following the death of Shuttarna II of Mitanni to shake off the Mitannian yoke.

Ashur-nadin-ahhe (*c.* 1393-1384 B.C.) sent an embassy to Amenophis III, and received twenty talents of gold from the pharaoh probably in the hope he would act as a check against Hittite expansion. *Eriba-Adad* I (*c.* 1383-1357 B.C.) assumed the title formerly used by Shamshi-Adad I of "governor of Enlil" which shows the growing self-consciousness of Assyria. After the murder of the powerful Tushratta of Mitanni, Assyrian forces joined those of Artatama from Hurri to invade Mitanni and divide among themselves the spoils. Suppiluliumas, king of the Hittites, intervenes and makes Mattiwaza, son of Tushratta, ruler over the buffer-state of Mitanni-Hanigalbat.

To the Assyrian throne now came *Ashur-uballit* I, the first of the great Assyrian kings of the Middle Kingdom. He was wise enough not to attack the Hittites to the west, while he strengthened his friendship with Egypt then ruled by Akhenaten. Encouraged by successes in the north, he invaded Babylon and placed on the throne the pro-Assyrian Kurigalzu II. His courtiers flattered him with the title of "king of the universe," and later sources speak of his restoration of the temple of Ishtar in Nineveh.

His grandson *Arik-den-ilu* left records of his military campaigns in the style of the Hittite reports. He fought in the upper region of the Tigris and the Zagros Mountains against Gutium, Kummuhi (Commagene), and the Turukku. Arik-den-ilu's son also reports that his father fought the Akhlame, which if correctly identified, would represent the first contact with the Arameans which would overrun Mesopotamia in the early part of first millennium. In the war against the Akhlame Arik-den-ilu used a contingent of ninety chariots.

Adad-nirari I, on the basis of the success of his father, expands the territory of Assyria to the south at the expense of Babylon, and to the west by incorporating the whole territory of Hanigalbat as far as Carchemish. As result of his successes he assumed the ambitious title of "king of the universe." Even his adversary the Hittite king Hattusilis III recognized in a letter the achievements of Adad-nirari.

Under *Shalmaneser I* (1265-1235 B.C.) Assyria had to make war on a new enemy, e.g., Urartu, burning fifty-one cities and carrying away the spoil. His next move was to reconquer Hanigalbat which had regained its independence with Hittite help. He made the whole territory a province of Assyria, and by deporting fourteen thousand soldiers of the enemy to Assyria broke for a long time the resistance of Mitanni. With this move Assyria became a neighbor of the Hittite Empire, even though King Hattusilis in his pride never recognized the new political standing of his enemy. Shalmaneser I was also engaged in a victorious campaign against the Quti to the east, and used the spoils of war to restore temples, and to build a new capital at Kalah, forty-five miles from Nineveh up the Tigris river.

Tukulti-ninurta I (1235-1198 B.C.) pursues for a while the expanding policies of his father, but conflicting interests in the court bring his career to a sad end, and Assyria sinks back into obscurity for a few decades. He starts his reign with a victorious campaign which in two years carries his triumphant army from Armenia in the north to the Persian Gulf in the south. He defeats Kashtiliash IV of Babylon, takes him captive to Assyria together with a statue of Marduk, levels the walls of Babylon and sets over it an Assyrian governor. Tuthalia IV, king of the Hittites, is upset with the triumphs of Assyria, but can do nothing more than blockade its commerce in Syria. Unexpectedly the warlike drive of Tukulti-Ninurta is spent, and he now directs his activities to the rebuilding of temples and palaces. He erects a new capital, Kar-Tukulti-ninurta, and fortifies it with walls and towers. He loses contact with the political situation, the nobility turns against him, and he is finally murdered in a palace revolution led by his own son.

The parricide *Ashur-nadin-apli* did not fulfill the hopes of the military party. On the contrary the energetic Kassite king Adad-shum-nasir got the upper-hand and made Assyria a vassal state for a while. After a few years another son of Tukulti-ninurta, *Enlil-kudur-usur,* was elevated to the throne, and he renewed the war against Babylon. Both the Assyrian and the Kassite kings died on the battle field, but the army was led back by the prince *Ninurta-apal-ekur* who became the next ruler in Assyria. But neither he nor his immediate successors carry the title of king, but only of "ensi of Ashur."

Meanwhile in Babylon the Kassite Dynasty is overthrown and replaced by a native dynasty known in history as the Second Dynasty of Isin. Babylon under *Nebuchadnezzar* I (c. 1128 B.C.-?) enjoys once again some days of glory. It was able even to impose a Babylonian ruler over Assyria who obligingly returned to Babylon the statue of Marduk which Tukulti-Ninurta had carried as a trophy many years before. Nebuchadnezzar I appears as an energetic king, who fought successfully against the Lulabeans, the rebellious Kassites, and Elam. Upon his victory over the troublesome Elamites he assumed the title "king of the universe." But the new power of Babylon was due more to the personality of Nebuchadnezzar I than to a real awakening of Babylonian life. Soon after his death Babylon relapses into a state of weakness.

In Assyria on the contrary *Tiglathpileser I* (c. 1116-1078 B.C.) carries to its height the military power of Ashur which had been awakened by Ashur-uballit and Adad-nirari, and promoted by Shalmaneser I and Tukulti-ninurta I. His exploits were the inspiration of the Assyrian despots who caused the world to tremble from the ninth to the seventh century B.C. Under him the Assyrian army became a war machine which knew no mercy, whose cruelty spread terror over its enemies even before they engaged in battle. Tiglathpileser I first directed his war effort against the Mushki in Asia Minor. In the words of the king, the blood of the slain flowed like torrents in the valley, and the heads of the enemy rolled from the cities like heaps of corn. After campaigning for four years in the west, he turned his efforts to the northeast to crush the lands of Nairi around Lake Van. The Hittite state of Malatia submits without fighting and pays tribute. He then carried a victorious raid to the Mediterranean, being the first Assyrian king to set foot on the Phoenician coast. He is deeply impressed by a live crocodile sent him by the pharaoh. The passage to the west was disputed over and over by the elusive Aramean hordes, and Tiglathpileser reports that he crossed the Euphrates twenty-eight times to subdue them. Assyria's repeated border violations of Babylonian territory finally led to open war in which king Marduk-nadin-ahhe was defeated and killed, and Babylon conquered. But age-old respect for the source of their common civilization kept Tiglathpileser from incorporating Babylon into Assyria.

When not engaged in war, Tiglathpileser spent time hunting lions, bisons and elephants in the region of the Upper-Euphrates. He collected exotic animals for his zoological garden, and planted a botanical garden. Rich with the plunder of scores of nations, he also employed his energy in directing the fortification of city-walls, erection or restoration of palaces and temples, and there is reason to believe that he created the first Assyrian library.

Nothing is known about the circumstances of the death of Tiglathpileser I. Under his successors Assyria again lost much of its power and prestige. Assyria seems to have exhausted its resources in the superhuman effort of making good the claims of their national god Ashur to world dominion. From *Ashur-nasirpal* I (1052-1033 B.C.) there is preserved a prayer in which after reporting his good deeds — rebuilding of destroyed temples, restoration of divine images — he confesses his sins, and asks why Ishtar does not heal the repentant petitioner from his infirmity. A tablet of a later king tells how Assyrian colonies in the Middle Euphrates had been lost to the Arameans. In fact it seems that the last few years of the second millennium witnessed the progressive infiltration of Mesopotamia by the hard-driving Arameans, while Assyria and Babylon lie powerless in the face of mounting danger.

19

THE NEW ASSYRIAN EMPIRE

When after some decades of obscurity the curtain rises again on the stage of Assyrian history, we find the Arameans firmly entrenched in Syria and Upper Mesopotamia, as well as in Babylon where the Aramean Adad-apal-iddina had usurped the throne about 1050 B.C. The related Chaldean tribes had in turn overrun Lower Mesopotamia. Only Assyria had the inner strength to resist the aggressive Arameans, and here in 932 B.C. a monarch ascended the throne determined to expand once more the power of Ashur. This was *Ashur-dan* II (932-910 B.C.) who can be credited with having been the renewer of the economic and military might of Assyria. He conceived as the first goal of Assyria to overthrow the growing Aramean power. This task which he pursued relentlessly, would long engage the best energies of his successors.

Greater than Ashur-dan was his son *Adad-nirari* II (909-889 B.C.). With him begin the new eponym lists which were found in the library of Ashurbanipal and which contain an uninterrupted series of eponyms down to the end of Assyrian history, thus allowing a firm chronology to be established. Eponym is the Greek equivalent of *limmu* who was the high officer whose name was given to the year. Usually an officer would enjoy the honor of being *limmu* only once in the reign of a king. Besides the name of the *limmu* the lists also mention in many instances the most important event of the year. It is easily seen how valuable such lists are to the modern historian.

Annals and building inscriptions tell of the campaigns of Adad-nirari against the lands of Nairi on the northeast, against Kummuhi (Commagene) in Asia Minor, and of his repeated expeditions against the Aramaized Hanigalbat and its capital, Nisibis. To capture Nisibis he built a trench and wall around the city. The city had to capitulate and Hanigabalt was made an Assyrian province. Adad-nirari also campaigned against the territory of Babylon, captured several cities, and made its king Nabu-shum-ishkun a prisoner. But out of respect for the old cultural and religious center, Adad-nirari instead of flaying his adversary alive as he had done with many others, makes a peace-treaty with Babylon cemented by a political marriage. The "Synchronistic History" reports, "Friendship and complete peace they made; the people of Assyria and Akkad lived together as trusting brothers." After this success Adad-nirari took the titles of "king of the universe, king of the four quarters of the earth."

It lies beyond the scope of this historical survey to deal minutely with the yearly campaigns undertaken by Assyrian kings in order to crush some rebellious territory or expand their empire, the report of which make up the bulk of the Annals. Assyrian monarchs seemed to be obsessed with the idea that their god Ashur demanded universal obeisance, even if this had to be exacted by the most cruel methods. They are never daunted by the difficulties of the terrain. Pity towards the vanquished enemy seldom enters into consideration. They follow a systematic policy of terror, and glory themselves in burning cities, flaying the most recalcitrant enemies, cutting off heads by the thousands, deporting women and children or burning them with the ruins of their city. This policy of terror and cruelty is interpreted by the Assyrians as a service rendered to their gods and particularly to Ashur, the god of thunder. But whenever there is a weak ruler on the Assyrian throne the subjected peoples take the opportunity to reassert their independence, forcing the Assyrian army to an endless series of campaigns which after some centuries exhausted the physical and economical resources of the nation, bringing about its downfall. On the other end it must be conceded that Assyria functioned as the watch-dog on the northern frontier protecting Mesopotamian civilization against the recurrent threat of barbarian invasion. Only when Assyria betrayed its trust as guardian and turned its military might against the heart of Mesopotamia in its unhappy relation with Babylon in the days of the Sargonids did she commit the unpardonable sin and nemesis overtook her.

The next great king who carried the tradition of Adad-nirari was *Ashur-nasir-pal* II (883-859). The records from this king allow us to see him first as the cruel warrior, who glories in the massacre of thousands of enemies, and then as the wise administrator, concerned with the welfare of his nation, who builds cities and temples, erects granaries, digs canals, directs the plantation of fruit trees, reforms the army, and raises a new capital, Kalah-Nimrud, the palace of which is adorned by artists from every place, to which flowed the wealth of many conquered nations. His palace was brought to light first in the middle of the last century by the excavations of Layard. New excavations carried in the same place by Mallowan since 1950 have again enriched our knowledge of Assyrian art and history with the discovery of new relief scenes, statues, and a new stela four feet high containing 154 lines of writing. The inscription records the campaign of Ashur-nasir-pal's first five years, the new founding of Kalah, the adornment of the palace, the erection of a golden life-size statue of the king before Ninurta, his care for the many temples, and the dedicatory feast of the palace to which five thousand foreign guests were invited besides sixty-five thousand craftsmen, palace officers and distinguished people of both sexes.

Ashur-nasir-pal II's military glory lay in the subjugation of the Arameans. When the city of Bit Halupe revolted, he put down the rebellion with a typical demonstration of Assyrian ruthlessness. In the Annals he reports that he built a tower opposite the city gate, captured the city, flayed the chief rebels and covered the tower with their skins; others he walled up inside the tower, or impaled on poles over the tower. The princes of Hattine and Carchemish hastened to send tribute and contingents of troops. When he marched on Phoenicia the cities of Tyre, Sidon, Gubla (Gebal), and Arvad immediately submitted. Then like Sargon of Akkad fifteen hundred years before, he washed his weapons ceremonially in the waters of the Mediterranean. After a few more campaigns he restored Assyria to the territorial greatness it had achieved in the days of Tiglathpileser I.

His successor *Shalmaneser* III (858-824 B.C.) faced the double task of preserving the territories gained by his father, and to expand them still farther. Dependent on plunder for its very life, Assyria would collapse economically should the war-machine stop its gruesome work. In spite of many setbacks he had the perseverance to pursue the goal proposed. He first directed his attention to the Aramean state of Bit Adini which he conquered after three campaigns. But when he tried to conquer Damascus he was faced by a coalition of twelve kings including Barhadad (Biblical Benhadad) of Damascus and Ahab of Israel. The engagement at Qarqar in 853 B.C. was a drawn battle, as it is clear from the fact that Shalmaneser did not return to this region until five years later. Only after the death of Ahab who fell in battle against the Syrians in Ramoth-Gilead, the assassination of Barhadad by Hazael, and the consequent weakening of the western coalition, was Shalmaneser able to impose tribute on most Syrian and Cilician states. It is remarkable that even Egypt furnished a contingent of one thousand soldiers to the western coalition against Assyria. Among those who twelve years later paid tribute to Shalmaneser was Jehu of Israel who among others is portrayed doing obeisance in the famous Black Obelisk of Shalmaneser.

Shalmaneser's advance to the north was brought to a halt by the resurgent power of Urartu. Victory stelae at the headwaters of the Tigris and the Euphrates mark the maximum advance of the Assyrian army. Toward Babylonia Shalmaneser preserved peaceful relations. Once he was invited to come to Babylon to

The Black Obelisk of Shalmaneser.
Courtesy, The British Museum

help the legitimate king against an usurper. Having re-established order he took the opportunity to extend his authority as far south as the Persian gulf. The Aramean states of Bit Amukkani and Bit Yakini hastened to send tribute of gold, ivory and elephant skins probably imported from India. Thus without touching Babylon, Shalmaneser was entitled to call himself "king of the four quarters of the world."

After 832 B.C. Shalmaneser III left the command of his military expeditions to his faithful general Dagan-ashur. From 827 B.C. on there were uprisings in the kingdom. Rivalries between two of his sons, Ashur-nadin-apal and Shamshi-Adad V, split loyalties in the court, and the old king retired to his palace in Kalah where he died a few years later.

In the following contest for the throne *Shamshi-Adad* V (832-810 B.C.) got the upper hand with the help of Babylon. Within three years he became master of the situation, but there is no question that the borders of the empire had been greatly curtailed. In a campaign Shamshi-Adad carried to the region of Lake Urmia princes of Media appear for the first time on the stage of history. The friendship with Babylon was suddenly broken when a new king, Marduk-balatsu-iqbi, came to the throne. The king of Babylon was defeated on the field of battle and captured. Many of his followers were flayed alive in Nineveh. A new king was placed on the Babylonian throne, Baba-ahi-iddina. But he did not meet Shamshi-Adad's approval, was defeated in battle and taken captive. Shamshi-Adad now advanced in triumph through Kutha, Babylon and Borsippa, and like his father received the tribute of the Chaldean-Aramean states on the Persian Gulf.

Since Shamshi-Adad V had died while the crown-prince *Adad-nirari* III (809-728 B.C.) was still a minor, Assyrian history presents the rare spectacle of a woman acting as regent for her son during four years. She was *Sammuratmat,* whom Greek legend later celebrated as Semiramis, and to whom they ascribed the construction of the "hanging gardens" of Babylon, a war against Africa and an expedition to India. What is true is that she gave good account of her regency, led the army with success to the north and west, and exerted a strong influence upon her son when he came to the throne. When Adad-nirari III assumed the reins of government conditions were so favorable that he was able to undertake a successful expedition to Syria-Palestine, as result of which Tyrus, Sidon and Israel (Land of Omri), Edom, Philistia, and Damascus submitted and paid tribute. By submission is not meant loss of territory but only willingness to pay tribute. Expansion to the north was now impossible because of the resurgent power of Urartu which had subdued the region of Lake Van, Parsuash and Malatia. In compensation the army made repeated incursions into the territory of Media in the northeast. Probably under the influence of his Babylonian mother, Adad-nirari promoted the worship of the god Nebo of Borsippa, to whom he erected a temple in Kalah. In his almost exclusive devotion to Nebo Adad-nirari seems to have approached a kind of henotheism.

Under the reigns of Adad-nirari's immediate successors, *Shalmaneser* IV, *Ashur-dan* III and *Ashur-nirari* V, who together reigned from 781 to 746 B.C. Assyria underwent another period of weakness. The most powerful figure in Assyria during this period was the commander Shamshi-ilu. He leads the army against Urartu, Matilu and the Syrian states. He crushes revolutions within Assyria itself. He arbitrates in matters of succession to the throne, and spends his last years as a virtual sovereign in Til Barsib, where two lion gates carry his inscriptions.

During the reign of *Ashur-dan* III occurred a solar eclipse the date of which when recalculated by modern astronomers furnished the year 763 B.C., which became the anchor of Assyrian chronology. A contributing cause to Assyrian impotence at this time was a terrible plague which devastated the country. This period of relative peace gave a breathing-spell to such nations as Israel which attained its maximum territorial expansion under Jeroboam II, and Judah which also enjoyed unprecedented prosperity under the long reign of Uzziah.

Under *Tiglathpileser* III (745-727 B.C.), who was placed on the throne by a military revolt, Assyria recovered its position as undisputed power in the Fertile Crescent. In nineteen years of constant warfare he built the empire anew. He practiced mass deportation in great scale, but when a nation submitted voluntarily he allowed it to retain its own rulers, as was the case with Gurgum, Hamath, Gubla, Tyre and Israel. To put an end once for all to the confusion in the relations with Babylon, Tiglathpileser united it to Assyria by making himself king of Babylon. As king of Babylon he assumed the name of *Pulu* by which he is known in the Babylonian Chronicle.

His most powerful rival was Sardur II of Urartu who had gained control of northern Syria. Tiglathpileser defeated him and his allies in a battle in the Upper Euphrates. Arpad, the capital of the disloyal Matilu, was taken after a three year siege and razed to the ground. In 738 B.C. he defeated a coalition of nineteen cities in the district of Hamath on the Orontes, and made Kullani (Biblical Calno) the capital of a new Assyrian province.

The most serious adversary of Assyria now was Rezin of Damascus. He allied himself with Pekah of Israel, and made war on Ahaz of Judah who refused to join the anti-Assyrian coalition. This is the so-called Syro-Ephraemite War the reverberations of which are echoed in Isaiah 7 and 8. Ahaz in desperation appealed to Tiglathpileser for assistance, sending him a sizable tribute. Tiglathpileser needed no second call. His army was soon on the march and Israel lost most of its territory except for a small district around Samaria. Probably with Assyrian connivance, Hoshea murdered Pekah, and assumed the throne as a vassal king. In 732 B.C. Damascus was conquered and Rezin met his death. The territory of Syria was incorporated as a province. The energetic Hanno of Gaza, one of the Philistine cities, paid for his resistance with the loss of his territory, and the destruction of his capital. He himself escaped to Egypt.

When Nabunasir of Babylon died, and the country became the prey of rival Aramaean chieftains, Tiglathpileser invaded the land, defeated the chief rebel Ukizer, and in 729 B.C., after "taking the hand of Marduk" in the temple of Esagila, according to ancient ritual, he made himself king of Babylon, in which capacity he became known as Pulu. Tiglathpileser now assumed the full title of "king of the universe, king of Assyria, king of Babylon, king of Sumer and Akkad, king of the four quarters of the world." When he died in 727 B.C. he left his son an empire of which he could proudly say that it stretched "from Bit Yakini (on the Persian Gulf) to the mountains Demawend (slightly to the south of the Caspian Sea), from the rising of the sun to the sea of the setting sun, unto Egypt."

At his death the scepter passed to his son *Shalmaneser* V (726-722 B.C.). When encouraged by Egyptian help Hoshea refused to pay tribute to Assyria, Samaria was promptly besieged, and in 722 B.C. fell into Assyrian hands. According to the Assyrian Annals 27,290 citizens of the better classes were deported to cities beyond the Euphrates, and peoples from other areas were settled in Samaria. From the intermingling of natives with the new comers resulted the Samaritan people whom the Jews despised because of their mixed blood and mixed religion. A revolt in Bit Adini was also crushed with ruthlessness. As king of Babylon Shalmaneser was named Ululai, a name not particularly flattering. But his career was cut short by a revolt of the conservative Assyrian party who, very likely, did not approve his lenient policies toward Babylon. Their leader on assuming the throne took the name of Sharrukin, "the Rightful King," (Biblical Sargon), and with him began the last brilliant phase of Assyrian history.

20

THE SARGONIDS—FALL OF ASSYRIA

Sargon II (722-705 B.C.) carried the military tradition of Tiglathpileser III forward. A succession of very able kings, a rather seldom occurrence in history, allowed Assyria to enjoy another century of power and dominance in the Near East. Thanks to very complete annals, mostly known in several recensions, and more than fourteen hundred letters from the archives in Nineveh, historians are exceptionally well informed concerning this period.

Sargon claimed for himself the conquest of Samaria, practically completed by his predecessor Shalmaneser V. With the deportation of thousands of citizens and the settlement in the territory of Samaria of new populations, the kingdom of Israel came to its end. A new attempt of Hanno of Gaza to set foot in southern Palestine with Egyptian help was defeated. A revolt of Hamath, with the support of Arpad, Simyra and Damascus was crushed. In 717 B.C. Carchemish, the last of the Hittite states on the Upper Euphrates, fell to Sargon. The kingdom of Urartu weakened by pressure from the Cimmerians was no longer in condition to resist the onslaught of Assyria. Its capital Tushapa was conquered in 714 B.C., king Rusa chose death rather than surrender, and an immense booty of war flowed to Assyria. In Asia Minor Kue (Cilicia) was subjugated, but the Mushki, very likely the Phrygians, under Mita their king, resisted further Assyrian penetration.

In Southern Mesopotamia the Aramaean princes refused to acknowledge Assyrian lordship. In 721 B.C. the Chaldean kinglet Marduk-apal-iddina (Biblical Merodach-Baladan) from Bit Yakini had made himself sovereign in Babylon. When in his second year Sargon tried to intervene he was defeated by an Elamite king in the battle of Dir. After ten years Sargon made a second attempt to control Babylon and this time he succeeded.

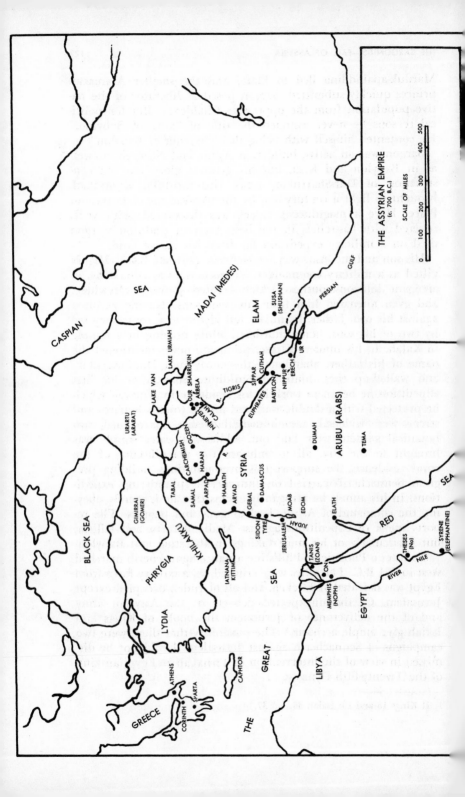

THE ASSYRIAN EMPIRE
(c. 700 B.C.)

SCALE OF MILES
0   100   200   300   400   500

Marduk-apal-iddina fled to Elam, and the smaller Aramaean princes quickly submitted. Sargon posed as liberator of the native population from the oppressive Chaldeans. But for political reasons he never assumed the title of "king of Babylon." He contented himself with being the "governor of Babylon."

Sargon was an active builder in Ashur and Nineveh, as well as in Babylon and Kish, but his greatest glory was the construction of Dur-Sharrukin, near the modern Khorsabad, brought to light a century ago by the excavations of Botta and Place. Here a magnificent palace was discovered, with walls covered with bas-reliefs in the best Assyrian tradition. Sargon died on a military expedition far from his native land.

His son and successor was *Sennacherib* (704-681 B.C.). Highly gifted as a military commander, Sennacherib was ruined by an arrogant self-consciousness which created hatred everywhere, and even alienated him from his own sons. Having revolted against his own father, he finally fell victim to a conspiracy led by two of his sons, being murdered while praying in a temple in Kalah. In his numerous inscriptions he never mentioned the name of his father, abandoned the newly-built Dur-Sharrukin, and walled-up the unfinished buildings. Soon after his first expedition he began to work in his residence in Nineveh which he protected with a double wall and fifteen towers. Squares and streets were widened, a monumental avenue was opened, two botanical gardens were laid out, additional water supply was brought to the city, all to enhance the magnificence of the royal residence. To support this over-ambitious building program Sennacherib carried on innumerous plundering expeditions. In his annals he arrogantly claims that he is merely obeying the command of Ashur, lord of gods and peoples. The reports speak of expeditions against Media, Urartu and Cilicia, but particularly of his undertakings in Palestine and Babylon.

To meet a Phoenician-Philistine alliance Sennacherib marched west in 701 B.C. The allies were crushed, an auxiliary force from Egypt was defeated at Eltekeh, and all of Judah occupied except Jerusalem. Of the unexpected debacle of the Assyrian army and of the deliverance of Jerusalem the books of Kings and Isaiah give ample account. [1] The possibility that there were two campaigns of Sennacherib against Jerusalem should not be dismissed in view of the intervention of Tirhakah an Egyptian king of the Twenty-fifth Dynasty.

---

1. II Kings 18 and 19; Isaiah 36 and 37.

Guardian deity from Sargon's palace at Khorsabad.
Courtesy, Oriental Institute

Palace of Sargon II at Khorsabad. Artist's reconstruction.
Courtesy, Oriental Institute

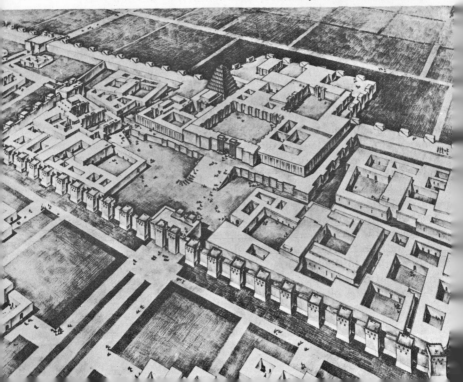

Captives and spoil from the city of Lachish.
Courtesy, S. H. Horn

Sennacherib's relations with Babylon were most unhappy. Since in his pride he failed to "take the hands of Marduk" in the Babylonian New Year festival, in order to assume the kingship officially, a certain Marduk-zakir-shumi, the "son of a slave," made himself a king. He in turn was expelled by the obstreperous Marduk-apal-iddina who had occupied the Babylonian throne for twelve years in the days of Sargon. Sennacherib drove Marduk-apal-iddina out after a short reign of six months, and put Bel-ibni on the throne who was supposed to be loyal to Assyria. Soon after he was involved in a revolt with Marduk-apal-iddina and other traditional foes of Assyria. Sennacherib intervened once more and placed his oldest son on the throne of Babylon. On the first opportunity Hallushu, king of Elam, conquered Babylon, took Sennacherib's son prisoner and placed a figurehead on the throne. Sennacherib took to the field once more, defeated Hallushu of Elam who soon afterwards met a violent death. Finally in 689 B.C. Sennacherib entered Babylon as conqueror, and now gave free rein to his wrath. The city was destroyed, the statue of Marduk, chief god of Babylon, removed to Ashur, the inhabitants murdered or deported, the temples razed and the "holy ground" loaded on ships and carried down the Euphrates to the island of Dilmun in the Persian Gulf. Over the ruins of the unhappy city Sennacherib had water channelled to erase all traces of its existence.

Little is known of the last years of Sennacherib. The Annals are silent. Concerning his end the Babylonian Chronicle reports: "In the month of Tebet, on the 20th day, Sennacherib, king of Assyria, was killed by his son in a conspiracy." He was succeeded by *Esarhaddon* (680-669 B.C.) .

Esarhaddon, also a son of Sennacherib, carried the imperial policies of Assyria to its farthest goal — the conquest of Egypt. But to achieve this he weakened the defenses of the northern borders where the Gimirrai (the Cimmerians) posed a constant threat. As an expiation for the violence done to Babylon by his father, he engaged in a program of rebuilding the city after receiving the kingship from the hands of Marduk. The temple-complex of Esagila together with its ziggurat Etemenanki "the house of the foundation of the heaven and the earth" were rebuilt, the city walls were repaired, the scattered citizenry was gathered and endowed with its old privileges. The Assyrian capital Ashur was also the object of his care and building activity.

His military campaigns were directed first against the Sea-land, in Lower Mesopotamia, whose king, a grandson of Marduk-apal-iddina, escaped only to be murdered by the Elamites. Next he fought against the Cimmerians, then against Sidon which was destroyed in 677 B.C. To offset the growing pressure of the Cimmerians, in response to an oracle, he gave his daughter in marriage to Vartatua, king of the Scythians, traditional enemies of the Cimmerians, who were now held in check.

With his rear-guard protected, Esarhaddon now felt strong enough to launch out on the conquest of Egypt. The Babylonian Chronicle reports briefly, "In the seventh year, in the month of Adar, on the fifth day the Assyrian army marched to Egypt." The expedition of 673 B.C. seems to have been stopped at the border by the army of Taharqo, a king of the Ethiopian dynasty. Before embarking on the second expedition Esarhaddon named his younger son Ashurbanipal coregent and heir of the whole empire, while giving to his older son the throne of Babylon. This was a grave political mistake with fatal consequences for the future of Assyria as we shall see.

After extensive preparations the army was on the march. Tyre made common cause with Egypt and was besieged, while the main body of the army marched to the south skirting the Mediterranean coast. Careful arrangements were made to provide water for the army while crossing the desert of Sinai. This time Taharqo was unable to resist the Assyrian onslaught, and the capital Memphis fell. The pharaoh escaped to the south, but his court and an immense booty were carried off to Nineveh. On a victory stela erected in Til Barsib Esarhaddon is depicted leading by a cord the crown-prince of Egypt, and Abdimilkutti of Sidon. This victory was also commemorated on a huge rock inscription near the river Kelb, in Syria, next to that of Ramesses II.

But in Assyria itself the victorious king had to face a complot of the aristocracy probably related with the succession to the throne. As a result many high-ranking officials were executed. Egypt revolted in the meantime and Esarhaddon decided on a third expedition to subdue it. But the ailing monarch died on the way, far from his home country, in October of 669 B.C.

According to his father's will *Ashurbanipal* (668- *c*. 631 B.C.), ascended to the throne. He was the last of the great Assyrian kings, equally gifted as a commander, statesman, hunter, art collector and passionate lover of antiquities. The library discovered by Rassam in 1854 in the ruins of his palace in Nineveh contained twenty thousand tablets, comprising the main works of Assyrio-Babylonian literature. In spite of the culture of which he prided himself so often, in war Ashurbanipal showed the traditional ruthlessness of the Assyrian monarchs. A captured Arab sheik was kept in a cage at one of the gates of Nineveh. Elamite princes had their lips cut off. Corpses of the citizens of rebellious cities were suspended on stakes around the conquered places. On the other hand he showed unexpected humanity to Neco of Egypt and to numerous pretenders to the Elamite throne.

In Egypt the interrupted expedition of his father was carried to a triumphant conclusion by the commander Shanabushu. As four years later Egypt revolted once more under Urdame (Tanutamun), the Assyrian armies returned in full strength and conquered Thebes in 663 B.C. The fall of Thebes of the "hundred gates" found repercussion even in the pages of the Bible. [2] With the heavy war-booty two large obelisks were carried off to Nineveh, together with a statue of Taharqo, discovered in 1955. Tyre after a siege of ten years submitted. So did Arvad, followed by the submission of all Syrian princes. The Anatolian states of Tabal and Hilakku sent tribute, and even Gyges, king of Lydia, dispatched a peace embassy. Assyria had attained the height of its power.

2. Nahum 3:8-10.

But the mighty empire was soon to be shaken to its very foundation by a general revolt led by Ashurbanipal's brother Shamash-shum-ukin who ruled as king of Babylon. He placed himself in 652 B.C. at the head of a coalition of the traditional enemies of Assyria: the Aramaean states, Gutium, the Arab sheiks east of Syria-Palestine, Lydia, Egypt under Psammetichus, and Elam. The civil war lasted four years and consumed the best energies of Ashurbanipal. Babylon was finally subdued and Shamash-shum-ukin perished in the flames of his palace. The city which had suffered much under the siege was spared further destruction, and a certain Kandalanu was placed on the throne of Babylon.

Ashurbanipal carried the war further, and invaded Elam which then received its death blow. Susa the capital was destroyed in 639 B.C., and Elamite history ceased until a century later it regained some luster under the Persian kings. The Arab tribes were castigated, but there was no effort to reassert Assyrian domination over Egypt which had revolted. Ashurbanipal used the remainder of his reign for building and literary activities, as well as to consolidate the empire which was weakened and impoverished after these prolonged wars. A curtain of obscurity falls upon the last years of Ashurbanipal. Not even the year of his death is known with certainty.

After his death the empire disintegrated rapidly. After the devastating civil war which ended in 648 B.C. the revenues of the empire were no longer sufficient to sustain the enormously expanded war establishment. The flower of the Assyrian manpower had also been consumed in the holocaust of unending wars. Assyria had over-expanded and her strength was no longer equal to the exacting task of maintaining so many peoples in submission.

Ashurbanipal's son *Ashur-etil-ilani* (c. 630-628 B.C.) was yet able to retain Babylon, and to repel the encroaching Medes under Phraortes. In 627 B.C. the usurper Sin-shum-lishir drove the weak king from the throne, but he himself was soon ousted by another son of Ashurbanipal, *Sin-shar-ishkun* (c. 627-612 B.C.) He seems to have possessed some of the energy of his father, but failed to recognize that the tide of history was now running against Assyria.

When Babylon revolted under Kandalanu, Sin-shar-ishkun was able to subdue it once more. But the Chaldean Nabopolassar now claimed the throne of Babylon, and his authority there became undisputed after 625 B.C. Nippur remained loyal to

Assyria, though. But the power of Media, greatly increased by the assimilation of the Cimmerians, was now alarming every nation in the Fertile Crecent. To face the common threat, Assyria, Scythia and Egypt made an alliance of mutual defense. When Cyaxares defeated the Assyrians in battle and besieged Nineveh, the Scythian army under Madyas came to its rescue. As a result the shrewd Cyaxares now directed his attention to the Scythians who were defeated in 616 B.C., while his ally Nabopolassar of Babylon obtained a victory over the Assyrians. Psammetichus I of Egypt now came to the assistance of Sin-sharishkun, and Nabopolassar was driven back. But in 614 B.C. Cyaxares conquered Ashur, and in July of 612 B.C., under a combined attack of Medes and Chaldeans, the venerable city of Nineveh fell. According to Greek tradition, Sin-shar-ushkin chose to die with his family in the burning ruins of his palace. Nineveh, Kalah and all important cities were razed to the ground never to be inhabited again. Such was the hatred which Assyria had engendered in all its neighbors, that nothing short of total obliteration could expiate it.

Only Harran, long since the western metropolis of Assyria, held its own. Here, after the fall of Nineveh, prince *Ashur-uballit* II assumed kingly power, and with Egyptian support was able to maintain himself for a few years. But in 610 B.C. Harran fell to the combined onslaught of the Medes and Chaldeans, and Ashur-uballit was forced to withdraw to northern Syria. An attempt to recover Harran the next year with Egyptian help failed. The colossus of Assyria which had been the scourge of the Near East for almost half a millennium came to its end. But no historian should begrudge the Assyrians the honor of having protected Mesopotamian civilization from barbarian invasions from the north for several centuries. Nor were they inferior to the Babylonians in artistic pursuits as the beautiful reliefs in their palaces abundantly reveal.

21
THE NEO-BABYLON EMPIRE

After the defeat and death of his brother Shamash-shum-ukin, Ashurbanipal had enthroned in Babylon a certain Kandalanu. Following the death of the powerful Ashurbanipal, Kandalanu tried to make himself completely independent, but was defeated by Sin-shar-ishkun. Under these conditions a new pretender to the throne of Babylon came to the front, namely Nabu-apal-usur, better known as *Nabopolassar* (625-605 B.C.). He took advantage of the declining power of Assyria to assert his independence. With disguised pride he called himself "a son of nobody," "whom Marduk had not seen among the people." As a Babylonian by birth he felt called by Marduk and Nebo to overthrow Assyria, and carry the tradition of the Chaldean Marduk-apal-iddina, who might have been one of his ancestors.

Since the Chaldeans were inferior to the Assyrians and Medes in military strength, Nabopolassar chose to achieve his objectives through diplomacy rather than through the power of arms. He made a treaty with Cyaxares, king of the Medes, defining their sphere of influence. Media would content itself with Northern Mesopotamia, leaving Nabopolassar free in Middle Babylonia and Syria. Of the participation of the forces of Nabopolassar in the destruction of the Assyrian Empire enough has been said in the previous chapter. His statesmanship is shown in the sending of the crown-prince and general Nebuchadnezzar to gain control of Syria after the conquest of Harran, before Pharaoh Neco II could consolidate his claim to the region. In 605 B.C. Nebuchadnezzar defeated the Egyptian army at Carchemish on the elbow of the Euphrates. The river was crossed and he obtained a second victory at Hamath on the Orontes. In consequence he quickly gained control of Syria and Palestine to the border of Egypt.

With greatly enlarged resources Nabopolassar was able to engage in the restoration of the sanctuaries of Babylon. As "king of Babylon, Sumer and Akkad" he glories in his work in the ziggurat of Marduk and the Etemenanki, which lay in ruins. He also rebuilt the outer wall of Babylon, and according to Herodotus, spanned a bridge over the Euphrates connecting the two sections of the growing city. Nabopolassar died after a reign of twenty years without seeing the full results of his military and building activities.

He was succeeded on the throne by his able son and co-regent Nabu-kudur-usur, "Nabo protects the border," the Biblical *Nebuchadnezzar* (605-562 B.C.) . Without doubt he was the greatest of the kings who sat on the throne of Marduk. In numerous building inscriptions he speaks with pride of his building activities in all the temples of the land, particularly of Babylon, where he restored the temple of Esagila, the Etemenanki, canals, walls, the processional avenue leading to the gate of Ishtar, etc. As a lover of antiquity he speaks of the rediscovery of some temples which had been completely covered with debris like that of Ebarra in Larsa, and of some old foundation stones, one of which must have belonged to Naramsin. For strategical reasons he built a wall to the north of Babylon closing a narrow gap between the Tigris and the Euphrates to protect the city against attacks from that quarter.

Following the precedent of the great Hammurabi and of Sumerian rulers in general, Nebuchadnezzar is very sparing in his inscriptions about military enterprises. He prefers the glory of being the good shepherd of his people. So for the several expeditions to Judah which led to the destruction of Jerusalem we have to turn to the *Chronicles of the Chaldean Kings* recently published by D. J. Wiseman on the basis of tablets found in the British Museum, or to reports in the Old Testament. These military campaigns have received ample confirmation through the *Lachish Ostraka* discovered in 1935 in the outskirts of ancient Lachish, through archeological excavations of many sites which show that these places were destroyed and remained unoccupied during the sixth century, and more recently by a papyrus found in Saqqara in 1942 and published by Dupont-Sommer, in which a certain Adon, probably the prince of Ashkalon, asks the pharaoh, very likely Apries (Biblical Hophra) , for help against the approaching Babylonians. According to the *Chronicles of the Chaldean Kings* Nebuchadnezzar fought a heated battle with Pharaoh Amasis in 601 B.C. In 597 B.C. he

Babylon in the Sixth Century B.C. The Ishtar Gate is in the foreground and the ziggurat appears on the horizon. Photo of painting by Maurice Bardin. Courtesy, Oriental Institute

stormed Jerusalem, carried King Joachin and his mother as hostages, and set Zedekiah on the throne. When nine years later Zedekiah revolted relying on the support of Pharaoh Hophra, the Babylonian army returned, and after a siege of eighteen months Jerusalem fell. Thus in 586 B.C. the kingdom of Judah came to its end. Zedekiah was taken to the presence of Nebuchadnezzar in Hamath, and after seeing his sons executed, was blinded and taken prisoner to Babylon. Judah was treated as a Babylonian province.

In 585 B.C. Nabuna'id (Nabonidus), a high-official who later became king of Babylon, negotiated a peace treaty between Media and Lydia fixing the river Halys as the boundary between the two kingdoms. After a siege of thirteen years Tyre which with Egyptian support had long resisted Babylonian control fell, but as the prophet Ezekiel said, its spoils were scarcely worth all the trouble Nebuchadnezzar had. [1] A fragmentary inscription mentions a military campaign against Amasis of Egypt in Nebuchadnezzar's thirty-seventh year.

Having elevated Babylon to be the "queen of the kingdoms," Nebuchanezzar died after forty-three years on the throne. His reign marked the apogee of the Neo-Babylonian Empire. His pride is the magnificence of Babylon, the splendor of which had already been praised by Herodotus, received fresh confirmation by the excavations of Koldewey in the ruins of the ancient city just prior to the first world war. The walls do not measure up to the exaggerated figures of Herodotus, but they encompassed an area of six square miles which easily places it first among the cities of antiquity. Less than twenty-five years after the death of Nebuchadnezzar his brilliant empire had fallen into Persian hands.

The scepter of Babylon was inherited by *Amel-Marduk* (561-560 B.C.), "man of Marduk," who had none of the ability of his father Nebuchadnezzar. Little more is known of him than is reported in the Bible, namely, that he granted amnesty to king Joachin of Judah who had languished in captivity for thirty-seven years. Some historians believe that he tried an anti-priestly policy and failed. He was driven from the throne by his brother-in-law *Nergal-shar-usur* (Biblical Neriglissar), who in his building inscription stresses his piety as "renewer of Esagila and Ezida," the two main sanctuaries of Babylon. Little is known of the four years of his reign, except that he directed a

---

1. Ezekiel 29:13.

military campaign across the Taurus, a mountain range separat-
ing Northern Mesopotamia from Asia Minor, in which he met
defeat. The rising power of the Persians under the leadership of
Cyrus now posed the main threat to Babylon.

Foreboding evil for the future of Babylon was the rift which
came about between the priests of Marduk in the capital, which
had been especially favored by the Chaldean kings, and the
Aramaic clergy of the cult of Sin whose worship centered in
Ur and Harran. When Nergal-shar-usur died after a short reign,
and was replaced by his son *Labashi-Marduk,* the priests of the
moon-god Sin grasped the opportunity to further their interests
by having Labashi-Marduk murdered, and placing on the throne
Nabonidus (555-539 B.C.) .

Nabonidus was a native of Harran, where his mother functioned as high-priestess of Sin. As such Nabonidus was first of
all a devotee of the moon-god, and paid only lip-service to the
other gods of Babylon. In one inscription he expressly says that
it was Sin and Nergal that appointed him to the kingdom from
birth. The best of his building activity he devotes to the temples
of Sin in Ur and Harran, and to the temples of Shamash in
Sippar and Larsa. Like Nebuchadnezzar he is also known by
his antiquarian interest, and in the course of restorations he
discovered the foundation stones of the temple which Urnammu
of the Third Dynasty of Ur had erected to Sin. It is not sur-
prising therefore that the priests of Marduk in Babylon greeted
Cyrus as a liberator, and composed a poem lambasting the
heretical king. But that no revolution was attempted during
the reign of Nabonidus attests to the firmness of his grasp in
political affairs. No idle dreamer was Nabonidus, but a shrewd
analyzer of the political scene.

In his foreign policy Nabonidus seemed to have obtained some
advantage by supporting Cyrus in his struggle against Astyages
of Media (550/549 B.C.) . Occupied with plans for a military
expedition against Lydia, Cyrus left Nabonidus free in the possession of Harran, the important caravan center in Upper Mesopotamia. Foreseeing that he would eventually have to measure
forces with Cyrus, Nabonidus fortified Harran as an emergency
capital, and tried to create a common Babylonian-Arabic front
against Persia by befriending the Arab sheiks and fixing his
residence in the oasis of Teima for eight years. Many ties of
affinity bound the Chaldeans and these Arabian tribes, of which
the worship of Sin was not the least. Besides shut up from the
ordinary trade routes to the east by Persia, Babylon had to

expand her trade with the west and south in order to survive. Hence the great interest in controlling the caravan routes which linked South Arabia and Syria. Economic interests led Nabonidus to establish garrisons and plant colonies as far south as Yatrib, modern Medina, on the Red Sea.

Meanwhile he placed his son *Bel-shar-usur* (Biblical Belshazzar) as co-regent in Babylon. Many original documents which have come to light in the last fifty years transferred Belshazzar from the realm of legend to that of well-established history. But the repeated omission of the New Year festival due to the absence of Nabonidus from Babylon helped to foster a growing discontentment. When he returned to Babylon to celebrate the New Year festival of 539 B.C. with great pomp, it was already too late. The feelings of the population were alienated. Gubaru, Nabonidus' governor of the territory of Gutium on the east of the Tigris, joined Cyrus. This act of treason marked the beginning of Persian aggression.

To strengthen his position Nabonidus brought the gods from all surrounding cities to Babylon. Borsippa, Kutha and Sippar refused to cooperate. In a battle at Sippar, Gubaru (Gobryas) forced the crossing of the river Tigris, and the Babylonian troops retreated in confusion. Two days later the Persians entered Babylon without fighting (October 12, 539 B.C.). We are particularly well informed of the events which took place thanks to two original documents, the "Chronicle of Nabonidus," and the "Cylinder of Cyrus," which though written by two antagonists agree very substantially. The aging Nabonidus who was in command of the army in Opis was taken prisoner, but soon after granted parole. There was no general pillage, and the temples were especially protected. Belshazzar must have perished in a palace skirmish, even though contemporary documents are silent about it. On October 29 Cyrus made his triumphant entry into Babylon, greeted as liberator. The city was treated with benevolence. The statues of the gods were returned to their respective shrines.

With the fall of Babylon, the ascendancy of the Semites in the Fertile Crescent ceased for a thousand years. Indo-European races would now carry the torch of civilization.

22
MEDIA AND PERSIA

1. Media

The territory occupied today by Persia (Iran) was first over-run by Aryan tribes coming from the region beyond the Caucasus in the middle of the second millennium B.C. Part of these tribes migrated all the way to India, while others settled on the territory to the east of Assyria, today known as the Iranian Plateau. Of these the Medes and Persians were to play the most important role in history. Both are mentioned for the first time in the annals of Shamshi-Adad V concerning Assyrian campaigns in the region of the Caspian Sea.

The Medes were the first to attain a measure of political organization at the end of the eighth century. According to Herodotus, *Deioces* was the first king of the Median clans, and the one who founded the capital Ecbatana. He was succeeded by his son *Phraortes,* who was active against the Assyrian Empire in the days of Esarhaddon. The growing power of Media was curtailed for a while by an invasion of the Scythians, very likely the Ummanmanda of the Babylonian sources, who dominated all of Iran for about a quarter of a century (653-625 B.C.).

Cyaxares (625-585 B.C.) wrested control of Media from the barbarians, and pushed Median power to its height. He made vigorous attacks against Assyria, and succeeded in capturing Ashur in 614 B.C. In alliance with Nabopolassar of Babylon he captured Nineveh in 612 B.C., thus destroying once for all the power of Assyria. He led his army in a victorious campaign into Asia Minor, crossing the river Halys, all but crushing the kingdom of Lydia. The peace-treaty concerted by Nabonidus between Media and Lydia was mentioned in the preceding chapter.

Under *Astyages* (585-550 B.C.), the Medians, now enjoying unprecedented wealth and power, soon lost their martial virtue.

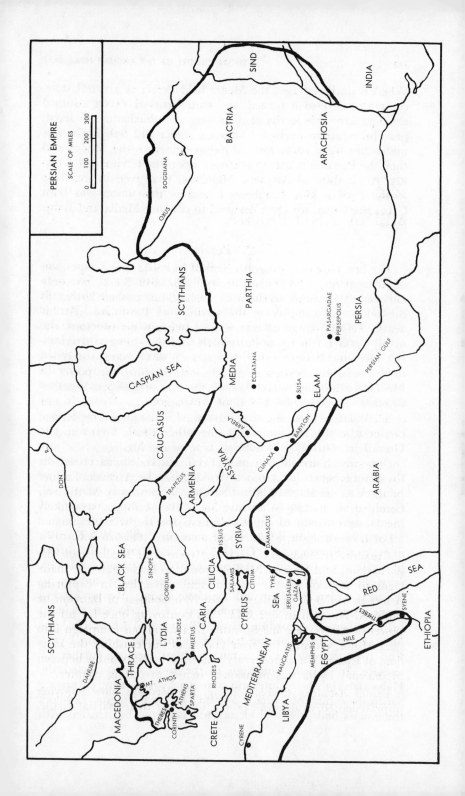

PERSIAN EMPIRE

SCALE OF MILES

0   100   200   300

Whereas until Astyages the Medes held Persia as a vassal state, the tables were soon turned, and with Cyrus II Persia assumed the dominant role in the east. As long as Nebuchadnezzar lived, peaceful relations prevailed between Media and Babylonia. But under the weak successors of Nebuchadnezzar the Medes and then the Persians began to encroach upon the territory of Babylon. A daughter of Astyages, Mandane, was given in marriage to the Persian king Cambyses I, and of this union was born Cyrus the Great, who was destined to conquer Media and Babylonia.

2. Persia

The first king to distinguish himself in Persia was *Teispes,* son of Achaemenes, who during his rule (675-640 B.C.), not only annexed the Elamite territory of Anshan, but pushed farther to the southwest, conquering the territory of Parsumash. At his death, Teispes' kingdom was divided between his two sons, the older, *Cyrus* I, inheriting Parsumash, and the younger, *Ariaramnes,* receiving Persia proper. But as soon as Cyaxares succeeded in defeating the Scythians, greatly strengthening the power of Media, the horizon darkened over the sons of Teispes. Whether Cyaxares annexed the realm of Ariaramnes to Media is not clear. What is sure is that the sons of Ariaramnes no longer carried the title of kings. On the other hand, Cyaxares left Cyrus I in control of Parsumash as a vassal king.

Cambyses I, second son of Cyrus I, succeeded his father on the throne, since his brother Arukku had been carried off to Nineveh as a hostage by Ashurbanipal. As previously mentioned, Cambyses I married Mandane, daughter of king Astyages of Media, and of this union was born Cyrus II the Great.

Cyrus II (559-530 B.C.), whose name in Persian was Kurush, in Hebrew Koresh, and in Greek Kuros, first occupied the throne of Persia as a vassal under Astyages of Media. But when after six years he was summoned to Ecbatana to render homage to Astyages, Cyrus rebelled and marched against Media. After a single engagement Media surrendered, and Cyrus was off on a brilliant career. According to the "Babylonian Chronicle," the Median army revolted and handed its sovereign over to Cyrus, who then marched to Ecbatana without meeting further resistance. In a swift campaign to the west, Cyrus crossed the Halys river in Asia Minor and beat the Lydian army, occupying Sardis the capital of Lydia in 546 B.C. Its king, Croesus, to whom the oracles had predicted victory was captured but treated with leniency. The defensive alliance between Babylonia, Lydia and Egypt proved ineffective. Lydia was divided and incorporated into the Persian Empire. Seven years later, in 539 B.C., Cyrus entered Babylon, after his general Gobryas had occupied the city without much opposition. He thus ended Semitic rule in the Levant, and absorbed the former realms of Media, Assyria, Lydia and Babylonia into the Persian Empire. Documents of Cyrus dispatched from Babylon are dated from the year the city was taken, thus evincing the importance he attached to the event.

Cyrus' benevolent policies are seen in the way he treated the conquered populations and their religion. There were no general massacres, nor desecration of shrines. As part of his general policy of treating all peoples as friends, Cyrus issued a decree in 537 B.C. for the return of the Jewish captives to their native land, and for the rebuilding of their temple. Several thousand availed themselves of the opportunity and returned to Palestine there to renew a Jewish national state.

Cyrus' Cylinder. The inscription describes the conquest of Babylon by Cyrus, and how the Persian king permitted the people living in Babylonian captivity to return to their homelands and to rebuild their temples.
Courtesy, British Museum

To ensure the northern frontiers of the empire, Cyrus embarked on a series of expeditions against the barbarians in the region of the Caspian Sea, dying of wounds in a battle against the Massagetae. His simple tomb near Pasargadae agrees well with his modest character. Plutarch tells that Alexander found the tomb violated by Polymarchus, and ordered the restoration of the same. The following inscription is supposed to have been engraved in the Greek language to replace the original one in Persian: "O man, whosoever thou art, and whensoever thou comest, for come thou wilt, I know, I am Cyrus, who founded the empire of the Persians. Grudge me not therefore this little earth that covers my body."

His oldest son and successor, *Cambyses* II (529-522 B.C.), inherited nothing of the broad-mindedness and greatness of heart of his father. Had he not died after a short reign, the empire of the Achaemenids might have perished with him. Cambyses began his reign by putting to death his brother and rival Smerdis, but did it in such an underhand method that nobody was convinced. He then undertook a careful campaign to conquer Egypt. After defeating Psammetichus III in the battle of Pelusium (525 B.C.), he occupied Memphis. But an army of fifty thousand Persians sent to annex the oasis of Amon perished in the desert. In his caprice he favored some Egyptian temples, while plundering others. He was particularly incensed against animal worship, and is said to have personally killed the bull Apis of Memphis. In his outbursts of insanity he killed his sister and wife Roxana, shot his son Prexaspes through with an arrow, buried twelve noble Persians alive, condemned Croesus to death, repented, and rejoiced that the sentence had not been carried out. On his way to Persia to subdue a revolt started by the usurper Gaumata who claimed to be the slain Smerdis, Cambyses died. One tradition reports that he committed suicide.

The usurper Gaumata who entered history as the *False Smerdis* was a devotee of the early Magian faith resolved to destroy Zoroastrianism, the official religion of the Persian state. Darius, a descendant of Teispes through the line of Ariaramnes, or so he claimed, led a conspiracy of nobles which deposed and killed Gaumata. *Darius* I was made king, and he reports in the famous Behistun (Besitun) inscription, written in Old Persian, Elamite and Akkadian, the long struggle in which he engaged to reassert royal authority in the face of a series of revolts which had broken out throughout the land. The inscription reads partly: "Nobody dared to say anything in regard to Gaumata, the Magian, until I came. Then I pleaded with Ahuramazda. Ahuramazda brought me help.... Then I killed with a few men that Gaumata, the Magian, and the men who were his chief retainers.... Nineteen battles did I fight. According to the will of Ahuramazda I slew them and took nine kings prisoners...." He took Babylon after a long siege, impaling three thousand of its leading citizens. After pacifying one after another of the rebellious states, Darius put off his armor, and displayed his great talent as administrator. He concerned himself with legislation, taxation, military service, commerce, communi-

ate of All Nations at Persepolis
Courtesy, S. H. Horn

cations, writing and language. He organized the oldest postal
service linking together the provinces with the central government. He spent thirty-six years consolidating his vast dominion
which extended from the borders of Libya and the Aegean coast
in the west to the river Indus in the east, and from the Black and
Caspian Seas in the north to the Indian Ocean in the south.

The last years of Darius were embittered by his war against
Greece. When the Greek cities on the eastern border of the
Aegean revolted against Persia and received aid from Sparta
and Athens, Darius declared war on Greece. After the maritime

disaster of 492 B.C. in which the Persian fleet was wrecked in a storm off Mount Athos, Darius prepared a second expedition which should cross the Aegean directly and land an invading army on the beach of Marathon. The invaders under the command of Datis and Artaphernes were defeated with heavy losses by the Athenians under the command of Miltiades on the memorable plain of Marathon in 490 B.C. While engaged in far-flung preparations for another attack on Greece, Darius I died in 486 B.C.

Xerxes (486-465 B.C.) who succeeded his father on the throne is to be identified with the Ahasuerus of Ezra 4:6. One of his first tasks was to subdue Egypt which had revolted against Persian domination. Early in 484 B.C. Egypt was reconquered, but instead of posing as king of Egypt, Xerxes reduced it to a satrapy. A revolt in Babylon in 482 B.C. was crushed by his best general and brother-in-law, Megabyzus. As result the city suffered considerably. The temple of Esagila with its ziggurat was torn down, the eighteen-foot statue of Bel-Marduk, weighing nearly eighteen hundred pounds of solid gold was carried off and melted down for bullion. Babylonia was incorporated into the satrapy of Assyria. His next task was to avenge the defeat suffered by the Persian army at Marathon in 490 B.C. In spite of extensive and careful preparation, the bulk of the Persian fleet which included contingents of Egyptian and Cyprian ships was routed in a naval battle in the bay of Salamis in 480 B.C., and the army which had devastated Athens was crushed in 479 B.C. in the battle of Platea. In the same year another Persian fleet was destroyed in the battle of Mycale, off the coast of Asia Minor. Within a few more years the last vestige of Persian control disappeared from Europe.

Even though the war against the Greeks was a total failure, the resources of his vast empire still enabled Xerxes to continue work on the monumental buildings which Darius had started in Persepolis. In fact most of the monuments brought to light by the spade of the archeologist in Persepolis may be traced to Xerxes. In 465 B.C. Xerxes was assassinated in his bed-chamber by a group of conspirators led by Artabanus. In the following struggle for the throne, his oldest son was slain by his brother Artaxerxes who occupied the throne.

Artaxerxes I (465-423 B.C.) was surnamed Longimanus, because his right hand was longer than the left. The empire exhausted in the long wars with Greece needed peace and a dynamic king to revitalize its whole structure. But Artaxerxes fell far short of this need. The satraps had become quasi-independent kings ready to revolt at the first opportunity. Artaxerxes' first task was to put down a revolt in Bactria led by his own brother Hystaspes. In Egypt a certain Inaros attempted with Greek support to make the Delta independent. A Persian army was dispatched under the command of Megabyzus who defeated the Egyptians and Greeks, and completely restored Persian authority. The name of Artaxerxes appears in the Canon of Ptolemy as a legitimate ruler of the land. It was in his days that Herodotus, the Greek historian, visited Egypt, and carried the impression of a land well governed.

In his seventh year Artaxerxes issued the decree recorded in Ezra 7 authorizing a company of Jews to return to their home land under the leadership of Ezra. Thirteen years later Nehemiah who held the position of cup-bearer of the king was sent as governor of Judaea with authority to rebuild the walls of Jerusalem.[1]

In the west Persia was losing ground continually. Soon after a treaty had been negotiated by Callias in 445 B.C., Thrace was lost to Persia, and a Greek fleet dominated the eastern Mediterranean. Cyprus remained under Persian rule, but signs of the break-down of Persian power were evident everywhere.

Xerxes II (423 B.C.), the lawful heir and eldest son of Artaxerxes I, had a short reign of forty-five days. He fell victim to the ambition of his half-brother Sogdianos who sought to make himself king. But another half-brother of Xerxes took the field against Sogdianos. This was Vahuka, called by the Greeks Ochos. In the ensuing struggle Ochos came out victorious, and assumed the throne under the title of Darius.

Darius II (Ochos) reigned from 423-404 B.C. Under his weak rule, the empire was repeatedly shaken by revolts. The first was led by his brother Arsites. The revolt was crushed, but the king lost prestige when he broke an oath not to execute Arsites. Revolts in Lydia and Media were also suppressed with much cruelty. It was during his rule that a Jewish colony located on the island of Elephantine in Upper Egypt had their temple destroyed by the natives offended by Jewish religious practices. Three years later (408 B.C.) they wrote a long letter to Bigwai, the Persian governor in Jerusalem, soliciting his aid in securing from Persia permission to rebuild their temple. But Persian hold on Egypt was slipping by this time, and the evidence of the Elephantine papyri seems to show that the colony ceased to exist

---

1. Nehemiah 2.

a few years later. In 404 B.C. Egypt regained its independence under king Amyrtaios. In this same year Darius II died without deciding the issue concerning his successor, whether it should be his oldest son Arsikas born before he was king, or Cyrus born after he became king, and the only eligible heir under Persian custom.

Arsikas in violation of precedent occupied the throne under the name of *Artaxerxes* II (404-358 B.C.) . Cyrus who was at the time a satrap over a territory in Lydia feigned loyalty by sending the regular tribute to the court, while plotting to dethrone his brother with the help of Greek mercenaries. Mustering an army of eleven thousand heavy armed soldiers and two thousand light armed hoplites, Cyrus advanced resolutely through Asia Minor, crossed the Cilician Gates without meeting resistance, forded the Euphrates on foot to everybody's surprise, and reached Babylonia. In the battle fought in Cunaxa (401 B.C.) the gallant Cyrus met his death, even though his forces proved themselves superior to those of his brother. Xenophon who led the retreat of the Greek forces through hostile territory left in his book "Anabasis" this testimony to Cyrus: "So died Cyrus; a man the kingliest and most worthy to rule all the Persians who have lived since the elder Cyrus." The "retreat of the ten thousand" made famous by Xenophon's masterpiece showed once more the internal weakness of the Persian Empire. Of the original army eighty-six hundred are said to have reached safely the shores of the Black Sea.

By the treaty of Antalcidas negotiated with Athens after the collapse of the Athenian Empire, Persia once more acquired rule over the east coast of the Aegean as well as over Cyprus. But Evagoras who had made himself king of Cyprus, opposed Persian domination, and after a prolonged war was left in control of the island. An attempt made in 374 B.C. to reconquer Egypt then ruled by Nectanebos I proved a failure. A general revolt of the satrapies of the west led by Datames floundered because of the rival ambitions of the members of the alliance. King Tachos of Egypt while leading an army into Syria in support of the revolters suddenly found himself deserted by his army, while Nectanebos II made himself king of Egypt with Persian consent. In the midst of court intrigues over the succession, Artaxerxes II (Mnemon) died after a long and lusterless rule of forty-five years.

Artaxerxes III (358-337 B.C.) , whose original name was Vahuka, lost no time in getting rid of all possible rivals. He is said to have slain eighty of his brothers in one day. He next subdued revolts in Asia Minor, Cyprus and Phoenicia, where in Sidon the inhabitants betrayed by their king chose to die in the flames of the city rather than surrender. Having assured his rearward from any possible attack, Artaxerxes III prepared to invade Egypt with the help of Greek mercenaries. Nectanebos II made a gallant effort to preserve the independence of his country. But his army was defeated in 342 B.C., and Egypt returned to the position of a Persian satrapy. He treated the unhappy country with the utmost cruelty. City walls were razed, temples plundered, and part of the population deported to Persia.

To Mentor, his best commander, Artaxerxes entrusted the pacification of Asia Minor. The harsh policies of Artaxerxes paid off, and the empire was rescued once more from the brink of disintegration. But palace intrigues, as so often in Persian history, brought to the front the eunuch Bagoas who hired a physician to poison the king and his older sons. In the meanwhile he spared the life of Arses the youngest son, intending to manipulate him in his own interest.

Arses (337-336 B.C.) showed himself no willing puppet in Bagoas' hands, and was put out of the way after a brief rule. Bagoas now chose another scion of the Achaemenian family to place on the throne. But his choice proved to be his doom, for the new king who took the name Darius resolved to be king on his own right, and quickly had Bagoas poisoned.

Darius III (336-331 B.C.) came to the throne of Persia in the same year that his arch-rival ascended the throne of Macedonia. Under different circumstances Darius III might have proved a capable administrator. But his ability was no match for the military genius of Alexander, nor were the Persian armies mostly composed of mercenaries of different nationalities a match for the highly trained Macedonian troops. Assuming the throne at the age of twenty, Alexander with characteristic energy lost no time in compelling the Greek states to recognize his leadership, and to rally behind his banner with the goal of conquering the Persian Empire. Hostilities began in 334 B.C., and after the three memorable battles of Granicus, Issus and Arbella, Darius III took refuge in flight only to be murdered soon after by his own officers. With dramatic swiftness Egypt and the whole Persian Empire fell under the control of Alexander.

Culture and Organization of the Persian Empire

The empire of the Achaemenids embraced more peoples and

much greater territory than any previous empire in the Near
East. Twenty-nine barbarian peoples living on its eastern border are mentioned in the Behistun Inscription by Darius I, besides the older populations of Mesopotamia and the West. Next
to the Persians stood the Medians who shared with them the
political leadership, though in a subordinate position. Ideally
the kingship was exercised in the name of Ahuramazda, the
good god, who stood on a much higher ethical plane than the
god Ashur of the Assyrians.

Darius the Great left the highest expression of Persian art in
the royal palace he built in the little town of Parsa, later called
Persepolis by the Greeks. It is even today the greatest architectural ruin to be seen in the Near East. But the main administrative center of the empire was in Susa, the old Elamite capital,
which Darius greatly embellished. Here the king had his winter
residence and treasury, and was surrounded by the Persian and
Median nobility. Here he held the "council of the seven," and
was under the protection of the thousand "immortals" who
formed his body guard. Among the high-officers of the palace
ranked the cup-bearer, a position once occupied by the Jew
Nehemiah, a chamberlain, a chariot-driver, a spear bearer, and
a scepter bearer. Very likely the royal chancellor whose duty was
to compose the political and diplomatic documents belonged to
the "council of seven."

The language of the chancery was Aramaic which had by now
become the *lingua franca* of the Near East. The use of Persian
in written form was limited to monumental inscriptions. It was
written in a cuneiform script composed of fifty-one syllabic signs.
In the days of Darius I the empire was divided into twenty administrative provinces, known as satrapies. A vigilant eye upon
the satraps was kept by royal inspectors who travelled accompanied by enough troops so they could act without delay if circumstances required.

The satraps were immediate representatives of the king with
power to levy tribute, to legislate, to command the local garrison, and to deal with neighboring peoples. Their court was a
diminutive copy of the royal court, and they took special delight
in possessing "paradises," that is, vast parks rich in wild animals
where they were wont to hunt.

The unity of this vast empire was further enhanced by
uniform jurisprudence, by a net of royal roads, a postal system
which served both government and business, a uniform currency,
and by the universal use of the Aramaic language and script. In

spite of all measures, this massive structure tended to disintegrate since there was neither a cultural or a spiritual bond of unity. Natural barriers and enormous distances contributed to make the satrapies more and more independent. And the increasing reliance on mercenary troops could only foreshadow the day when the artificial colossus would collapse under the blow of a small but intelligent enemy.

The Religion of Zoroaster

Zoroaster is the Graecized form of the name of Zarathustra, the prophet of dualism in Persia. The content of his faith is known mainly from the book Avesta, the written form of which dates from about 200 B.C. Zoroaster himself is believed to have been active about the seventh century B.C. According to his teaching the only god is Ahuramazda, the wise lord. He alone is to be worshiped. Even though a monotheist himself, Zoroaster was unable to explain the existence of evil, and this difficulty gave rise to later dualistic interpretations in which the good god Ahura Mazda is confronted by the evil spirit Ahriman, the creator of evil. Zoroaster appears as a prophet and not as a lawgiver, or definer of the cultus. His attitude towards sin is not clearly defined, but Greek tradition has it that he laid emphasis on truth in speech and deed. His eschatology presupposes a real life beyond the grave, and a glorious consummation, with the total triumph of Ahuramazda. Stress is given to the ethical life, with recognition of the brotherhood of man and the duty of kindness toward animals, whose kinship with man is recognized. In the more developed dualism man finds his goal in life by joining the forces of good and thus hastening the ultimate triumph of light over darkness.

23
THE ARAMAEANS

The earliest reference to Aram as the name of a region or state is to be found in a cuneiform inscription of the Akkadian king of Naram-Sin of the twenty-third century B.C. It seems to place them in Upper Mesopotamia. The name *Aramu* appears in a Mari text of about 1700 B.C. Much later is an inscription of the Assyrian king Arik-den-ilu who speaks of victories over bands of *Akhlamu*. Tiglathpileser I declares that he had routed Aklamu-Aramaeans who came from the desert to cause unrest in Mesopotamia. These early references depict the Aramaeans as nomads on the verge of passing from the outskirts of the desert into the settled regions of the Fertile Crescent.

Taking advantage of Assyrian weakness during the eleventh and tenth centuries, the Aramaeans founded in northern Mesopotamia a series of little states, the chief of which being Bit Adini, with Borsippa for its center, and Bit Bakhyani, with Guzana (Tell Halaf) as its capital. Likewise on the shores of the Persian Gulf several Aramaean states were founded, the most important of which was that of Bit Yakini. *Bit* means "house," so these different states are named "house of so and so," and represent powerful clans united around some leading personality.

In their expansion to the west the Aramaeans founded in Cilicia the principality of Sam'al. In Syria we find the principality of Bit Agushi around Arpad and Aleppo. Farther south they organized themselves into the principalities of Soba and Damascus, about which we are better informed thanks to their contact with the Hebrew kingdom. Thus in II Samuel 10 we read of the Syrians of Beth-rehob (Bit Rahab) and Zobah (Soba) who allied themselves with the Ammonites against David, but were defeated by Joab the commander of David's army.

With the Assyrian revival in the ninth century the Aramaeans were gradually dislodged from their territories in Upper Mesopotamia. Shalmaneser III claims the conquest of Bit Adini in 856 B.C. But when he tried to subdue the Aramaean principalities in Syria he was opposed by a strong coalition in which Benhad of Damascus and Ahab of Israel were the chief figures. The battle of Qarqar in 853 B.C. proved indecisive, but twelve years later Shalmaneser III inflicted a defeat on a second alliance of Aramaean states, which, as a result, began to pay tribute to the Assyrian king as attested by the Black Obelisk.

To this period belongs the inscription in which Kilamuwa, king of Sam'al, records his victories over his neighbors, and the stela erected by Zakir, king of Hamath, to celebrate his victory against his enemies allied under the leadership of Damascus.[1] A century later Tiglathpileser III defeated a certain Azriyau who as a usurper had made himself king of Sam'al. The usurper was put to death and the throne restored to the legitimate king Panamuwa II, whose son Bar-Rekub recorded these happenings in his inscriptions.

Border warfare between the Aramaean state of Damascus and Israel dates back to the days of Ahab. After a brief alliance to face the common threat posed by Assyria, hostilities reopened over the control of Ramoth-Gilead, and in the ensuing battle in 853 B.C. Ahab lost his life.[2] In the days of Jehoahaz son of Jehu, the Israelites fared so badly in the hands of the Syrians that their army was reduced to no more than fifty horsemen, ten chariots, and ten thousand footmen.[3] Under the powerful king Jeroboam II the tables were reversed, and Israelite control extended over Damascus and even over Hamath on the Orontes. With the revival of Assyrian power in the middle of the eighth century both Damascus and Israel faced a mortal danger. Rezin of Damascus and Pekah of Samaria allied their forces against the common foe, trying in the meanwhile to force Judah to join in a common front. All to no avail. Tiglathpilesr III would brook no resistance. Israel lost most of its territory, and Damascus after a two-year siege was taken in 732 B.C.

Closely related to the Aramaeans were the Chaldean tribes who in Babylonia led a series of anti-Assyrian revolts, particularly under Marduk-apal-iddina, who succeeded in occupying the throne of Babylon for twelve years in the days of Sargon II.

---

1. Pritchard, *Ancient Near Eastern Texts*, pp. 500, 501.
2. I Kings 22.
3. II Kings 13:7.

Temporarily checked by the Assyrian might, the Chaldeans made a second bid for the control of Babylon, and under Nabopolassar and his successors established the Neo-Babylonian Empire.

Ever divided into rival petty states, the Aramaeans played a rather insignificant political role in the total picture of the Ancient Near East. But the decline of their political importance coincided with the spreading of the Aramaic as the *lingua franca* in the Fertile Crescent for many centuries. Thanks to its simpler script, Aramaic gradually permeated the Levantine world, and finally replaced Akkadian as the language of diplomacy and commerce. Innumerous finds of contracts, receipts and inscribed weights testify to the widespread use of Aramaic throughout the Near East.

An Aramaic papyrus first published by Dupont-Sommer in 1948, contains a letter from a Phoenician prince to the pharaoh, probably datable to 605 B.C., in which he asks for help against the oncoming Babylonians. A century before, the emissaries of Sennacherib to Hezekiah of Judah were asked to speak in Aramaic since the Jewish high officials on the walls of Jerusalem could understand it well enough.[4]

As Persia extended its rule from the Euphrates to Egypt including the whole Syro-Palestinian coast, the resulting amalgamation of culture raised Aramaic to the status of official language in the whole area. Phoenician and even Hebrew were superseded by Aramaic, and in the days of Ezra there was already felt the need to translate the Scriptures into Aramaic for the benefit of the common people. Originally this was only an oral rendering of the Hebrew text, but in a later period these paraphrases crystallized into the written Aramaic Targumin of different sections of the Scriptures.

The advent of Hellenism, with its cultural conquest of the Near East, caused a decline in the popularity of Aramaic, partly compensated by its adoption by the pre-Islamic states of Petra and Palmyra. Later under Roman rule, "from being the language of Christ, Aramaic became the official language of the Syrian Church,"[5] of which the greatest monument is the Syriac Bible, known as the Peshitta.

About the time of Christ two branches may be distinguished in Aramaic. One is the Western Aramaic represented by several

---

4. II Kings 18:26.
5. S. Moscati, *Ancient Semitic Civilizations*, p. 173.

dialects: Nabatean of the Petra inscriptions, Palmyrene of the Palmyra inscriptions, Judaean Aramaic represented by the Targumin, the Jerusalem Talmud and the Midrash. The other branch, Eastern Aramaic, which diverged more from Imperial Aramaic, is represented by Syriac, the language of the church of Edessa, by the language of the Babylonian Talmud, and by Mandaean, the language of the Gnostic group of that name.

From the days of the Persian Empire dates the literary work known as "The Story of Ahiqar," which came down to us in papyri of the fifth century B.C., but whose text probably goes back to the preceding century. To the story is appended a series of sayings attributed to the wise man Ahiqar, which consist of proverbs and fables, some of which may have found their way into Greek through the fables of Aesop. The flavor of his proverbs may be caught from the following excerpts:

> My son, chatter not overmuch, utter not every word that comes into thy mind. . . . Above all other things set a watch upon thy mouth, and over what thou hearest harden thy heart. For a word is a bird: once it is released none can capture it. . . .[6]

---

6. Pritchard, *Ancient Near Eastern Texts*, pp. 426-428.

24

THE ISRAELITES

Politically speaking Israel played a minor role in the history of the ancient Near East. Its diminutive territory, no more than one hundred miles from north to south, and fifty miles from east to west, allowed it no great political ambition. But in the history of religion its contribution was unique. The Old Testament stands as a monument to the religious genius of this people, and remains the major source of information concerning the rise and fall of the Israelite nation.

The Exodus

The Israelite tribes first became a nation at the Exodus, that is, at their going out of Egypt under the leadership of Moses. There is a great deal of disagreement as to the date of the Exodus, but few scholars are inclined to deny its authenticity, since this epic event left an indelible impression upon the religious thinking and political tradition of Israel. If I Kings 6:1 is taken literally, the date of the Exodus would fall about 1400 B.C. according to the following reasoning: the date when the Northern Kingdom under Jeroboam separated from the Southern Kingdom under Rehoboam occurred in 931 B.C. according to Thiele, or 922 B.C. according to Albright. The schism took place presumably in the year Solomon died. Since he reigned forty years, and the construction of the temple began in his fourth year, we must add 36 years to 931 to obtain the date when the foundation of the Solomonic temple was laid, namely, 967 B.C. Adding to this date 480 years we obtain 1447 B.C. as the date of the Exodus, and 1407 B.C. as that of the conquest of Jericho.

The British archeologist John Garstang, on the basis of excavations he carried on in Jericho and the near-by cemetery in the thirties, thought he had found evidence that the destruc-

Excavations at Old Testament Jericho are seen in the foreground, with the traditional site of the temptation in the background.

Courtesy, Religious News Service

tion of the city by the Israelites under Joshua took place no later than the days of Amenophis III (1413-1377 B.C.) of the Eighteenth Dynasty, or roughly about 1400 B.C. This evidence has been contested by Kathleen M. Kenyon who opened new trenches in the ruins of Jericho in the early fifties, and arrived at the conclusion that all strata later than 1600 B.C. had been eroded away. In this case there would be no trace of the fortified city conquered by Joshua.

Those who favor a date for the Exodus in the first quarter of the thirteenth century point to the fact that the reference to the store-cities of Pithom and Raamses [1] built by the Israelites while under Egyptian slavery agrees better with the political circumstances prevailing during the reign of Ramesses II (1301-1234 B.C.). Since the book of Numbers refers to established kingdoms in the Transjordan, namely, the kingdoms of the Moabites and Ammonites, through whose territories the Israelites had to cross, and since surface explorations carried on for two decades by Nelson Glueck showed little or no trace of sedentary life in that region until the thirteenth century, some see in this another evidence that the Exodus took place in the thirteenth rather than in the fifteenth century B.C. But even the evidence collected by Glueck is being contested by more recent research, so that the actual date of the Exodus better be left as an open question.

What preceded the Exodus was the age of the patriarchs. The Israelites trace their descendance from Abraham who migrated from Ur in Lower Mesopotamia to Harran in the north, and from that caravan center eventually into Canaan. Arabs claim descendance from Abraham through Ishmael, whereas the Israelites claim it through Isaac. Isaac, according to Genesis, was the father of Jacob from whom issued the heads of the twelve tribes of Israel. In light of recent research, particularly the discovery of the Nuzian tablets which threw light on the Hurrian customary laws, the story of the patriarchs emerges as credible and true to color. It fits well in the milieu of the Middle Bronze Age in the Fertile Crescent.

The book of Genesis concludes with the entrance of Jacob and his clan into Egypt on the occasion of a great famine. That Asiatics moved into Egypt as caravaneers, or in times of stress, is well to be expected. Midianites were employed in the copper mines of the Sinai Peninsula by Egyptian kings since the very first dynasties. On the tomb of a nobleman found in Beni Hasan is depicted a caravan of Asiatics entering Egypt on asses carrying tinker's bellows and musical instruments. That no written documents, no inscription whatsoever, have been found in Egypt referring to the Israelites should cause no surprise. To the mighty pharaohs this would have been regarded as a minor event unworthy of particular notice.

Asiatics would have been particularly welcome in the days of the Hyksos who ruled Egypt for about a century, between 1680 and 1580 B.C. The Hyksos being Asiatic invaders them-

---

1. Exodus 1:11

selves would favor the settlement of a new group of Semites which might lend them support in the struggle for the control of the country. The Hyksos' capital was Avaris on the eastern Delta, and .the narrative in the book of Exodus suggests that the land of Goshen was a fertile territory not far from the capital. With the expulsion of the Hyksos by king Amosis of the Eighteenth Dynasty, the Israelites would have lost their favored status and reduced to slavery.

Eventually under the leadership of Moses they left the land of their servitude under circumstances that for them always bore the stamp of divine interposition. After a month's march the tribes encamped by Mount Sinai, and there underwent a religious experience which welded them together into a nation, bound to Yahweh by a divine covenant. All subsequent history of Israel was irrevocably influenced by what took place at Sinai. Israel became conscious of being a "chosen nation."

Period of the Conquest

The first reference to Israel on any monument is found on the stela of Merenptah (Marniptah), in which the pharaoh claims victory over several Canaanite cities, and then states that "Israel is left a widow." It has been remarked that whereas the other proper names contain the determinative for city or land, that of Israel has only the determinative for people. At any rate it is clear that by 1200 B.C. Israel is in possession of at least part of Canaan, probably the hill-country which rises a few miles east of the shores of the Mediterranean. The story of the conquest is contained in the books of Joshua and Judges. Not prepared to conquer the land by a thrust from the south, the Israelites made a long detour through the lands of Edom and Moab, and after many vicissitudes crossed the Jordan from the East. The fall of Jericho opened the way for the conquest of central Palestine, the territory around Shechem, from where expeditions were directed first towards the south and then towards the north.

The glowing report of the book of Joshua must be balanced by the more factual narrative of Judges which makes clear that the valleys, particularly that of Jezreel, and many fortified cities were not immediately conquered. The Promised Land was not an empty territory waiting for the first comer. It was rather occupied by a number of city-states, each with its king, in constant warfare among themselves, owing a token fealty to

Egypt. Rapacious Egyptian officers and nobility had reduced the population to abject poverty, as witnessed by the ruins of Tell Beit Mirsim, excavated by W. F. Albright, in which there were found a few substantial buildings contrasting with the meager houses of the peasantry. Under the circumstances it is not to be surprised if the bulk of the population felt no urge to resist the invading Israelites. On the contrary the break-down of the old order might hold the brightest hope of a happier day for the freedom-loving peasants languishing in half serfdom. This was, for example, the case with the Gibeonites who chose to cast their lot with the invading Israelites.

The Period of the Judges

Until the establishment of the monarchy in the days of Saul, the strongest tie binding the Israelite tribes on both sides of the Jordan was the bond of a common religious faith and a common tradition. Except for this, "every man did what was right in his own eyes." Their religious fellowship centered in the sanctuary first located in Shiloh in the territory of the tribe of Ephraim. There a simple structure, if not the portable tabernacle itself which the Israelites carried during their wanderings in the wilderness, sheltered the ark of the covenant in which, according to tradition, were kept the tables of the law. The ark placed in the most holy compartment of the sanctuary was regarded as the visible throne of Yahweh. Priests claiming descent from Aaron, brother of Moses, offered sacrifices according to a prescribed ritual, and ministered to the religious needs of the people. Yearly feasts, such as the Passover celebrated in the spring and the feast of Tabernacles commemorated in the fall, attracted to the sanctuary representatives from all the tribes thus counteracting the centrifugal forces which tended to isolate the tribes from each other. The religious ties which bound the Israelite tribes around a common sanctuary were not dissimilar to the amphictyonic leagues which united the Greek city-states in common loyalty to a religious center like that of Delphi, for example.

After the partial conquest of the land, the first major threat to the Israelites came from the Philistines which had settled on the southeast corner of the Mediterranean shore after their unsuccessful attempt, along with other Sea-peoples, to conquer Egypt c. 1200 B.C. According to the prophet Amos, the Philistines came from Caphtor which most scholars identify with

Crete.[2] Pottery found in the excavation of Philistine cities tends to confirm this identification. One of the great ironies of history is that the name of the Philistines became forever attached to the Promised Land of which they occupied only a small fringe. Thus the land of Canaan is known to historians as Palestine.

The first major victory of the Philistines over the Israelites took place in Aphek in the days of the high-priest Eli, whose two sons were slain, the sanctuary in Shiloh destroyed, and the ark taken as a trophy of war. What gave the Philistines a decided advantage over the Israelites in this and subsequent encounters was the possession of iron weapons and a unified command. As late as the days of Saul, the record says, "there was no smith to be found throughout all the land of Israel."[3] The Iron Age had not yet dawned for the Israelites.

What kept Israel from total disaster was the strong moral leadership given to the nation by Samuel, the last and greatest of the judges. Judges were charismatic leaders who in times of national crises rose under divine compulsion and summoned his

2. Amos 9:7.
3. I Samuel 13:19.

Two prisoners from among the Philistines are brought to Rameses III who celebrates a victory by carving a relief on the walls at Medinet Habu.
Courtesy, Oriental Institute

distraught countrymen to action against the enemy and then to moral reform. Legends of uncommon bravery grew around such names as Othniel, Gideon, Samson and Jephthah. Samuel is better known as a prophet and founder of prophetic guilds, and the one who anointed Saul king.

Establishment of the Monarchy

The break with the tradition of theocratic government was not achieved without a rift in the national conscience. Some conservative elements like the Rechabites never ceased from looking upon the monarchy as a breach of the Sinaitic covenant. The conflicting currents of thought are reflected in the accounts of I Samuel 8 and 9.

Saul was from the tribe of Benjamin, a small but warlike tribe, and established his headquarters in Gibeah where a modest palace has been uncovered by archeologists. The new king with the support of several able commanders like Abner, his uncle, Jonathan, his son, and his son-in-law David, kept the Philistines at bay for several years. But jealous over the growing popularity of David, Saul drove himself insane. Instead of pushing the war vigorously against the Philistines, Saul engaged in an ignominious pursuit of David around whom a group of guerrilla bands steadily increased. Saul's reign ended with a disastrous victory of the Philistines over the Israelites on Mount Gilboa in which Saul and his three sons lost their lives. This battle may be dated *c.* 1010 B.C.

Acclaimed king first by the men of his own tribe, David reigned in Hebron during seven years, while Ishbaal, a surviving son of Saul, with the support of Abner, wielded a shadowy rule over the tattered remnant of Israel from Mahanaim beyond the Jordan. Convinced of the futility of further hostilities between the troops of Ishbaal and those of David, Abner made overtures to the king in Hebron for a peaceful settlement which would recognize David as sole ruler over the divided nation. But before the provisions of the treaty were set in operation, Abner had been murdered, and so had Ishbaal. With the last obstacle removed David assumed the rulership over all Israel.

In a master stroke of statesmanship David chose Jerusalem for a capital. It was still in the hands of the Jebusites, and by its central position could not arouse the jealousy of either party. The stronghold of the Jebusites was conquered by the indomitable Joab, commander of David's army, who apparently made use of a secret underground passage leading water from the spring of Gihon to a deep shaft within the city walls.

The first task confronting David was that of dislodging the Philistines from their positions in the hill-country to the north of Jerusalem. This he accomplished in two major engagements. His next concern was to make Jerusalem the religious as well as the political capital of the united kingdom. To this end he had the ark removed in a solemn procession from Kiriath-jearim, where it had been enshrined after the destruction of Shiloh, to the city of David. Here it was placed in a modest tabernacle pending the day when it would be translated to a temple commensurate with its sanctity. In spite of costly preparations, David never had opportunity to erect the temple he so fondly planned. It fell to his son Solomon, who lived in a more peaceful period, to carry out this project.

In a series of successful campaigns David definitely broke the power of the Philistines who ceased to pose a threat to the Israelites for two centuries. Likewise the Moabites who were settled in the territory east of the Dead Sea were defeated in battle and forced to pay tribute. More ambitious was the war David waged against Hadadezer, king of Zobah, who at the time held sway over Damascus as well. Hadadezer was defeated in two engagements, and an Israelite garrison was stationed in Damascus. Next to suffer the brunt of David's army were the Edomites in the south who controlled the profitable caravan routes which connected Arabia with Syria and the Phoenician ports. More troublesome were the Ammonites to the northeast who allied themselves with the Syrians in order to resist the onslaught of Joab's army. It was during the siege of Rabbah, modern Amman, capital of Transjordan, that the incident between David and Bathsheba, the wife of Uriah, an officer in Joab's army, took place. After a protracted siege Rabbah fell, and among the spoils was counted the royal crown weighing one talent which was placed on David's head. David's kingdom had attained its greatest territorial extent and to Jerusalem flowed the wealth of neighboring nations.

Adopting the polygamous habit of eastern monarchs, David brought upon himself untold woes as the sons of his many wives vied with each other for the throne. Amnon, the eldest, was put out of the way by the ambitious Absalom, third in line of succession. Exiled from the kingdom and later allowed to return at the instance of Joab, Absalom started a rebellion chiefly with the support of the northern tribes. After almost toppling

David from the throne, Absalom was defeated and killed in battle, but the seeds of discontent persisted. Not until the defeat of Sheba, a Benjaminite, who exploited the old sympathies for the house of Saul, did the kingdom attain again a semblance of unity.

David's hesitancy in declaring publicly his legitimate successor provoked another *coup* for the crown shortly before his death. This time Adonijah with the support of Joab, commander of the army, and of Abiathar, one of the chief priests, made secret arrangements to have himself proclaimed king. Hearing of the plot, Nathan, the prophet, and Zadok, the priest, took quick steps to have David appoint Solomon as the rightful heir to the throne. With David's blessing Solomon was made to ride the king's mule thus publicly displaying his right of succession. As news of the popular acclamation of the new king reached Adonijah's camp, his plot collapsed. Not long thereafter he lost his life at the hands of Benaiah, who succeeded Joab as commander of the army.

Solomon's Reign

Solomon's reign was marked at first by external peace and unprecedented prosperity. The greatly increased revenue resulting from the caravan trade and varied commercial enterprises, among which a royal monopoly of copper smelting, and of the commerce in horses and chariots between Cilicia and Egypt, allowed the king to indulge in a vast building program. This included first the erection of a magnificent temple to replace the old tabernacle which housed the ark of the covenant. To this end cedar of Lebanon was imported from Phoenicia by a trade agreement with Hiram, king of Tyre, who also provided skilled craftsmen to supervise the construction. Blocks of limestone were quarried not far from the chosen temple area on a hill in the northeast area of the city, where today the Mosque of Omar stands. Solomon's attention was next directed to the building of his own palace, the halls of which were panelled with cedar. Next to the palace stood the armory which came to be known as the "house of the forest" because of its colonnade of cedar beams supporting the roof. Archeological work in Jerusalem itself has been greatly hampered by continual occupation of the site, and as a result none of the buildings mentioned has been substantiated by actual excavations.

As foreign trade did not provide enough income to the expenses of a luxurious court, the country was divided into twelve districts for the purpose of taxation. The worst fears concerning the burdens a king would impose on the nation began to be realized. Discontentment seethed among the northern tribes never wholly identified with the house of David. The peasantry looked nostalgically back to the days when no tribute weighed upon their property to sustain an extravagant court alien to their democratic upbringing.

The Schism of the Northern Tribes

The banner of revolt was raised by Jeroboam, an Ephraimite, who occupied a responsible office in the royal administration. Forced to flee to Egypt, Jeroboam sought protection under Shishak, a pharaoh of the Twenty-second Dynasty, who himself was biding time to raid Palestine at the first opportunity. When Solomon died his kingdom was under the double threat of foreign invasion and internal strife.

When his son Rehoboam ascended the throne (931 B.C.), he was immediately faced with a general rebellion of the northern tribes under the leadership of Jeroboam who returned from his Egyptian exile. Unwilling to reduce the burden of taxation as demanded by the representatives of the nation, and impotent to stem the wind of revolt, Rehoboam saw himself confined as ruler of the tribes of Benjamin and Judah, while the ten northern tribes rallied under the banner of Jeroboam. Intermittent warfare ensued, but the rift in the political fabric was final. From then on the northern section would be known in sacred history as the Kingdom of Israel, while the southern portion, centered in Jerusalem, formed the Kingdom of Judah.

For the sake of convenience we shall first trace briefly the history of the Kingdom of Israel. Jeroboam's first concern was to break the attachment felt by every Israelite to the temple in Jerusalem. With this in view he erected two golden bulls as symbols of the deity, or, according to some, as pedestals upon which the deity was thought to be enthroned. A priesthood was appointed to offer sacrifices and carry on the prescribed services in the sanctuaries at Bethel and Dan where the bulls were enshrined. How far this innovation satisfied the religious aspirations of the common people is an open question. What is certain is that the Israelites exposed to a closer contact with surrounding nations quite early adopted a religious syncretism in which Yahweh was first among many gods. Chief rival of Yahweh in popular affection was Baal, a deity worshiped mainly in Phoenicia as patron of agriculture.

Naturally not every Israelite bowed his knee to Baal. A crisis shook the nation in the days of the prophet Elijah, whose name characteristically meant "Yahweh is my God." Elijah's ministry fell in the days of king Ahab who married the imperious Jezebel, daughter of Ethbaal king of the Sidonians. It was the deliberate policy of Jezebel to stamp out the cult of Yahweh from her realm, and to make the cult of Baal supreme. After a contest with the priests of Baal on Mount Carmel, near the Phoenician border, Elijah with popular consent executed several hundred heathen priests. But the issue remained undecided for lack of royal support until the conspiracy of Jehu (c. 841 B.C.), who massacred all scions of the house of Ahab.

Ahab's father Omri receives scanty notice in the Biblical record, but his political influence must have been considerable since in the Assyrian Annals the land of Israel is consistently referred to as the "land of Umri." It was Omri who built Samaria on a strategic mound and made it the capital of the kingdom, a position which it occupied until its destruction in 722 B.C. Ahab appears in the annals of Shalmaneser III as siding

Remains of the city gate of Samaria (cf. II Kings 7:1, 16-20).
Courtesy, Matson Photo Service

with the enemies of Assyria in the drawn battle of Qarqar (853 B.C.). As the Assyrian threat faded, the western alliance broke apart, and Ahab thought opportune to wrest Ramoth-Gilead from the hand of the king of Syria. In the ensuing battle Ahab lost his life.

Twelve years later we find Jehu, who had usurped the throne in a bloody revolution in which Ahab's son Joram was murdered, paying tribute to Shalmaneser III as depicted on the now famous Black Obelisk which today stands in the British Museum. Jehu had none of the political acumen of the Omrite dynasty, and Israel drifted in a few years into a position of utter helplessness before the kings of Damascus. Not until Jeroboam II (793-753 B.C.) did Israel regain its lost prestige. Jeroboam made the best of the opportunity offered him by the weakness in which Assyria fell during the first half of the eighth century. He enlarged the borders of his territory to its maximum extent, and gave the Israelites a period of prosperity such as they had not enjoyed since the days of Solomon.

The death of Jeroboam II marked the end of the last brilliant phase of the northern kingdom which now rapidly marches to its ruin. It would be idle in this short survey to review the reigns of the petty monarchs who now follow one another upon the throne of Samaria in rapid succession. Pekah who as sole king ruled from 740 to 732 B.C. joined in an alliance with Rezin of Damascus to resist the onslaughts of the Assyrian Tiglathpileser III. Unable to force Ahaz, king of Judah, to join their alliance, they embarked upon what is known as the Syro-Ephraimite war of disastrous consequences. Alarmed Ahaz appealed to Tiglathpileser for help, supporting his plea with a bountiful tribute. Tiglathpileser more than willingly accepted the call and marched against Rezin and Pekah. Damascus after a siege of two years fell to the conqueror in 732 B.C. Its territory was made an Assyrian province. The kingdom of Israel lost Galilee and the territory of Bashan east of the Jordan, and a large segment of the people suffered deportation to Mesopotamia. Pekah was murdered in a conspiracy, apparently with Assyrian connivance, and Hoshea ascended the throne. As long as Hoshea paid tribute to Assyria Israel was left in peace. But in 725 B.C. he succumbed to the temptation of sending an embassy to Sais (Biblical So) in Egypt, asking for military support, while he takes up arms against Assyria. Shalmaneser V promptly besieges Samaria which falls after a grim siege in 722 B.C., thus bringing to an end the existence of Israel as an independent state. Again, several thousand Israelites are deported to eastern lands, and the territory of the northern kingdom is made an Assyrian province.

The Kingdom of Judah

Rehoboam (931-913 B.C.) was the king in whose days the schism between Israel and Judah took place. After some feeble attempts to reunite the whole country Rehoboam had to resign himself with the rulership over Judah and Benjamin. With greatly curtailed revenues, the kingdom of Judah never attained the material prosperity of Israel which occupied a much larger and more fertile territory. To make matters worse, in the fifth year of Rehoboam's reign Shishak of Egypt made a plundering raid on the country carrying away much wealth accumulated in the days of Solomon.

Rehoboam was followed on the throne by Abijam, and he in turn by Asa (911-869 B.C.). In his days Zerah "the Ethiopian," probably a garrison commander posted by Shishak, or his successor Osorkon I, in southern Judah near the Egyptian border, took the field against Asa. The armies met near the border fortress of Mareshah, with the result that the Ethiopians were defeated and pursued till Gerar on the edge of the Sinaitic desert. Threatened later by Baasha king of Israel, Asa appealed to Benhadad king of Syria. Benhadad acquiesced and in turn raided the border territories of Israel, whereupon Baasha desisted of further interference with Judah.

Asa's successor Jehoshaphat (873-848 B.C.) inaugurated a religious reform in the country encouraging among his subjects the sole worship of Yahweh. But quite inconsistently he made a marriage alliance with Ahab of Israel which had calamitous consequences for his own dynasty. He fought side by side with Ahab in the battle for the reconquest of Ramoth-Gilead (853 B.C.), in which Ahab lost his life. Jehoshaphat escaped unscathed, but a few years later his kingdom was threatened by a coalition of Moabites, Ammonites and Edomites. According to the Chronicles, the invading armies destroyed each other, and Judah had but to collect the spoils. Jehoshaphat ranks among the good kings in the Chronicler's estimate chiefly because of his zeal for the Mosaic faith.

In the blood-purge which Jehu executed against the house of Ahab (841 B.C.) not only Joram of Israel and his mother Jezebel perished, but Ahaziah a grandson of Jehosphaphat as well. Athaliah, a daughter of Ahab and Ahaziah's mother, now conceived the sinister plan of murdering all the royal family of Judah, and seating herself on the throne. Joash, a son of Ahaziah, a mere child, was hidden by his aunt with the help of the high-priest and escaped the massacre. Six years later Jehoiada the priest led a revolt which deposed Athaliah and re-established the Davidic line with Joash on the throne. But neither Joash nor his son Amaziah brought any luster to the realm.

Only with Azariah (791-740 B.C.), also known as Uzziah, did Judah again enjoy a period of relative prosperity. Uzziah was energetic enough to capitalize on this period of Assyrian weakness to enlarge the borders of his country at the cost of the Philistines and Arabs. According to II Kings 14:22 he even regained control over the port of Elath at the head of the Red Sea, and which must have played an important part in the caravan trade. Its importance as a copper refining center has been contested more recently. The new wealth derived from trade and agricultural pursuits enabled Uzziah to expand the army, to outfit it more thoroughly than ever before, and to fortify Jerusalem with the newly invented catapults.

It was in the halcyon days of Jeroboam II of Israel and Uzziah of Judah that the first prophets of whose messages we have a written record made their appearance. Amos leaves his flocks in the wilderness of Tekoah, and goes to Bethel where the royal shrine of Israel was located there to pronounce his memorable indictments against the social evils of the day, exposing the folly of a religion divorced from morality. While his main stress was on God's demand for righteousness, Hosea out of the depths of personal experience was revealing to Israel the mercy of God which could not let the nation go in spite of its estrangement from Him. Somewhat later we find the prophet Micah championing the cause of the oppressed in Judah, and decrying the greed of those who add house to house and field to field "until there is no more room." A contemporary of Micah was Isaiah the prophet-statesman who elbowed with kings, and who denounced unrighteousness in high and low places. They were the forerunners of that worthy line of spiritual leaders whose faith and vision helped the Jewish people to survive the vicissitudes of exile, and to bless the world with a precious legacy of spiritual understanding.

Uzziah's long reign was followed by a period in which the heavy hand of Assyria began to be felt with increasing power. Tiglathpileser III (745-727 B.C.) in a few short years restored Assyrian ascendancy all over the Fertile Crescent. It was he who at the behest of Ahaz, a grandson of Uzziah, made a campaign against the Syrians and the Israelites and conquered Damascus in 732 B.C. Ahaz bought the independence of Judah by paying a heavy tribute to the Assyrian monarch, but the specter of Assyrian invasion loomed always above the horizon during the next half a century, and decidedly affected the foreign policy of the little kingdom.

Greater than Ahaz was his son Hezekiah (716-686 B.C.) who, presumably under the inspiration of the prophet Isaiah, inaugurated a religious reformation which purged the country from the grossest forms of heathen practices. The fact that people from Ephraim and Manasseh were invited to partake in the Passover celebrations in Jerusalem shows that the mass-deportation of captives which followed the fall of Samaria in 722 B.C. was not so complete as commonly conceived, and that the old hostility between the northern and southern tribes had practically melted in the fire of national disaster.

In the year of 701 B.C. Sennacherib of Assyria made a campaign against a coalition of western nations, among which Hezekiah was the most prominent. After subduing the rebellious Philistine cities by the Mediterranean shore, Sennacherib turned his forces against Judah, and overwhelmed forty-six of its fortified cities. Chief among these was Lachish, the most important defense to the south of Jerusalem. That Sennacherib regarded this an important victory is shown by the fact that a bas-relief was made on one of the walls of Sennacherib's palace in Nineveh to commemorate the event. In this the king appears sitting on a throne near the walls of Lachish receiving the submission of the elders of the city. Hezekiah was besieged in Jerusalem "like a bird in a cage," to use the expression in one of Sennacherib's inscriptions. Ready to appease the king, but unwilling to surrender Jerusalem, Hezekiah sent a heavy tribute to Sennacherib who was still in Lachish. The Biblical account says that the city was miraculously delivered, while Sennacherib nowhere claims the conquest of Jerusalem. Herodotus, incidentally, refers to a plague of rats which destroyed the strings of the bows and the leather of the shields of the Assyrian army when engaged in a war with Egypt at some such time. It is conceivable that a bubonic plague may have been responsible for the rout of the Assyrians who withdrew to their country without having fully accomplished their objective. The dogma of the inviolability of Jerusalem so fixed in the Jewish faith after the time of Isaiah is bound with the historicity of this incident. In this brief sur-

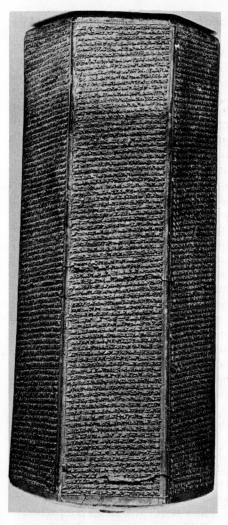

Taylor Prism, annals of Sennacherib.
Courtesy, British Museum

vey it is not possible to consider the merits of the two-campaign theory by which some scholars try to reconcile the Biblical data with the mention of Tirhakah of the Ethiopian dynasty who was too young to intervene in the events of 701 B.C.

Hezekiah was succeeded by Manasseh (696-642 B.C.) who in his lengthy reign undid much of the reformatory work undertaken by his father. The Chronicler attributes the latter woes suffered by the Jewish people to the outrages practiced by Manasseh against the national faith. He is reported to have spent some years as a captive in Assyria, later to be unexpectedly restored to his throne in Jerusalem.

The brief reign of Amon, the son of Manasseh, was followed by that of Josiah (640-609 B.C.), the last great king to sit on the throne of Judah. Like his great-grandfather Hezekiah, Josiah inaugurated a thorough program of religious reform which he extended to the cities of the former kingdom of Israel. There is reason to believe that taking advantage of the helplessness of Assyria after the reign of Ashurbanipal, Josiah tried to exercise actual political control over the remnant of the northern tribes. At least there is no hint of opposition to his reformatory activity in the territory formerly controlled by Samaria. The trend towards centralization of the cult in Jerusalem to avoid abuses in the minor shrines of the country received a great impetus from the discovery of "the book of the law" in Jerusalem by people engaged in the cleaning and repairing of the structure. The danger of amalgamating the Mosaic faith with heathen practices was always great outside Jerusalem, as evinced by the discovery of a Jewish colony in Elephantine in Upper Egypt. It presents the sorry spectacle of colonists there worshiping Anath-El and Beth-El side by side with Yahweh, early in the sixth century B.C.

For reasons which we can only surmise, Josiah regarded his duty to oppose Pharaoh Neco II when this monarch moved his army across Palestine in order to support Assyria in its death-struggle with Babylon in the year 609 B.C. What is sure is that Josiah could not look complacently upon an Egypto-Assyrian victory which would have left Judah at the mercy of Pharaoh Neco. In the unequal engagement at Megiddo Josiah lost his life. In the midst of general consternation, his body was brought to Jerusalem to be honored with a royal burial.

Judah had good reason to lament the death of Josiah, for the last twenty-two years of its life as a nation were marked by a series of disasters. Though failing to secure Harran for Assyria, Neco was able nevertheless to exercise sovereignty over Syria and Palestine for a few short years. Josiah's son Jehoahaz who had been placed on the throne was summoned to appear before the pharaoh on his return from Harran. He was deposed and taken prisoner to Egypt. Jehoahaz' brother Jehoiakim was appointed to succeed him, while Judah remained under Egyptian vassalship. Four years later Nebuchadnezzar of Babylon felt strong enough to challenge Egyptian supremacy over the western provinces of the defunct Assyrian empire. A major battle took place at Carchemish on the elbow of the Euphrates in 605 B.C. in which Neco II was thoroughly defeated. A second defeat of the Egyptians at Hamath on the Orontes brought the whole of Syria and Palestine under Babylonian suzerainty. Pressed to return to Babylon because of the death of his father, Nebuchadnezzar contented himself with receiving a token submission from Jehoiakim while carrying some hostages to guarantee the new settlement.

Jehoiakim of whom the Biblical record has little good to say remained loyal to Babylon only so long as circumstances forced him to do so. After the indecisive battle fought near the Egyptian border between the armies of Neco II and Nebuchadnezzar in the year 601 B.C., Jehoiakim apparently thought the time opportune to rebel. It was a fatal mistake which led to his own death in 597 B.C., and the conquest of Jerusalem by the armies of Nebuchadnezzar three months later. Jehoiachin who had replaced his father on the throne was captured and deported to Babylon together with his mother, high officials and several thousand of the leading citizens. The king's uncle Zedekiah was installed as a ruler of the shattered nation.

Ration lists for Jewish prisoners in Babylon.
Courtesy, Staatliche Museen zu Berlin

Judah was bent on its own destruction in spite of the warnings of the prophet Jeremiah who since the days of Josiah had been calling for a thorough spiritual reform as the only way to avert impending doom. But a blind reliance upon the inviolability of Jerusalem made the people deaf to the voice of the

prophet. Within a few years Zedekiah, his oath of loyalty to
Babylon notwithstanding, was steeped in rebellion with the
promise of Egyptian support. The response of Babylon was swift.
Jerusalem was besieged, the outlying fortresses of Judah taken
one by one, as reflected in the Lachish letters, an army sent by
Pharaoh Hophra to relieve the siege defeated, and the city
stormed after little more than a year. Zedekiah was captured as
he tried to escape with part of his troops, and brought in chains
to Riblah before Nebuchadnezzar. His eyes were gouged out,
and he was deported to Babylon with the tattered remnants of
his people. The fortifications of Jerusalem were dismantled,
her gates burned down, and only the poorest of the land left "to
be vinedressers and plowmen." Thus in 587 B.C. the kingdom
of Judah ceased to exist, its territory being annexed to the neighboring province of Samaria.

That the Jewish people did not lose its identity in the upheaval of the exile must be ascribed to its imperishable spiritual
heritage. To this none contributed more than the prophets who
since Amos raised their voice in protest against the moral degra-
dation which made of religion a mockery, enunciating in the
process those religious principles which sustained the soul of
the nation in the trying days of the captivity.

After the Exile

With the conquest of Babylon by Cyrus in 539 B.C., Semitic
supremacy in the Near East came to an end. The magnanimous
Cyrus inaugurated policies altogether different from those of
Assyria and Babylon. It was Cyrus' conviction that an empire
ruling over so diversified races and cultures could not long survive without the good will of the subjected nations. To achieve
this end Cyrus allowed complete freedom of religion within
the borders of the empire. In line with this policy he issued a
proclamation permitting the Jews to return to their native
land if they so desired. Several thousand Jews embraced this
opportunity to return and rebuild Jerusalem which still held a
high place in their esteem. Those who chose to return by no
means represented the majority, but they certainly embodied
the most religious segment of the population who were determined to uphold the traditional faith.

To their disappointment the returnees found living conditions in Judah quite disheartening at first. Most of the old
cities were in ruins, roads were at the mercy of brigands, food
supply was scanty and uncertain. Under the last weak rulers of

Babylon law and order must have broken down in the western provinces of the empire, and it would take time for the salutary effects of the Persian administration to be felt. But under the leadership of Jeshua the high-priest and of Zerubbabel the governor they undertook the rebuilding of the temple in Jerusalem in the face of much local opposition, particularly of the Samaritans still moved by old jealousies. In this task the people were greatly heartened by the exhortations of the prophets Haggai and Zechariah, so much so that by the year 515 B.C., in the sixth year of the reign of Darius I, a modest structure stood in the place of the old temple as symbol of Israel's faith.

In the reconstruction of the new social and religious order an important role was also played by Ezra and Nehemiah whose activities extended over the second half of the fifth century. The exact order of events as narrated in the books of Ezra and Nehemiah is a matter of dispute among scholars, but there is no question that their influence was weighty in stamping upon the new Jewish community its basic religious character. Empowered with a broad mandate from Artaxerxes I, Ezra set out with characteristic zeal to regulate the religious life of the nation according to the "law of his God," and even intervened in civil affairs, such as the matter of mixed marriages. Narrow-minded as these measures might seem to a modern reader, they were essential to preserve the status of the Jews as a unique race with a unique religious heritage. Ezra, the "scribe par excellence," is credited by Jewish tradition with a major responsibility in the establishment of the canon of the Old Testament, that is, of the authoritative collection of books which were regarded as divinely inspired.

Nehemiah's commission also granted by Artaxerxes I gave him the powers of a governor for all practical purposes. His main task was to rebuild the walls of Jerusalem and to place the civil administration of the little state on a firm footing. In conclusion it may be said that the Jews enjoyed a fair measure of religious and political freedom under the Persian rulers. But to pursue their history beyond the days of the Persian Empire is outside the scope of this short survey.

SELECTED BIBLIOGRAPHY

W. F. Albright, *From the Stone Age to Christianity* (rev. ed., Doubleday Anchor Books, 1957).

James Bakie, *A History of Egypt* (New York: The Macmillan Company, 1929).

J. H. Breasted, *A History of Egypt* (New York: Charles Scribner's Sons, 1959).

——————————, *The Conquest of Civilization* (New York: Harper & Brothers Publishers, 1926).

John Bright, *A History of Israel* (London: S C M Press Lts., 1960).

W. F. Edgerton, *The Thutmosid Succession* (The University of Chicago Press, 1933).

Jack Finegan, *Light from the Ancient Past* (Princeton University Press, 1959).

H. Frankfort, *Ancient Egyptian Religion* (New York: Columbia University Press, 1948).

——————————, *The Birth of Civilization in the Near East* (Bloomington: Indiana University Press, 1948).

Ignace Gelb, *Hurrians and Subarians* (The University of Chicago Press, 1944).

O. R. Gurney, *The Hittites* (Penguin Books, Inc. 1952).

H. R. Hall, *The Ancient History of the Near East* (London: Methuen & Co. Ltd., 1920).

B. Hrozny, *Ancient History of Western Asia, India and Crete* (Prague: Artia, 1953).

D. D. Luckenbill, *Ancient Records of Assyria and Babylonia* (The University of Chicago Press, 1926-27).

Sabatino Moscati, *Ancient Semitic Civilizations* (London: Elek Books, 1957).

M. Noth, *The History of Israel* (2d ed., Eng. tr., A. & C. Black, Ltd., 1958).

A. T. Olmstead, *History of Assyria* (New York: Charles Scribner's Sons, 1923).
————————, *History of the Persian Empire* (The University of Chicago Press, 1948).

James B. Pritchard, *Ancient Near Eastern Texts* (Princeton University Press, 1955).

M. Rostovzeff, *A History of the Ancient World,* Vol. I (Oxford: Clarendon Press, 1930).

R. W. Rogers, *A History of Ancient Persia* (New York: Charles Scribner's Sons, 1929).

H. H. Rowley, *From Joseph to Joshua* (London: Oxford University Press, 1950).

H. W. F. Saggs, *The Greatness That Was Babylon* (New York: Hawthorn Books Inc., 1962).

A. Scharff und Anton Moorgat, *Ägypten und Vorderasien im Altertum* (München: Verlag F. Bruckmann, 1959).

Hartmut Schmökel, *Geschichte des Alten Vorderasien* (Leiden: E. J. Brill, 1957).

Sydney Smith, *Early History of Assyria* (London: Chatto & Windus, 1928).

E. A. Speiser, *Mesopotamian Origins* (Philadelphia: University of Pennsylvania Press, 1930).

G. Steindorff and K. C. Seele, *When Egypt Ruled the East* (University of Chicago Press, 1947).

J. W. Swain, *The Ancient World, Vol. I* (New York: Harper & Brothers, 1950).

Merrill F. Unger, *Israel and the Aramaeans of Damascus* (London: James Clarke & Co. Ltd., 1957).

Arthur Weigall, *A History of the Pharaohs,* Vols I and II (New York: E. P. Dutton and Company, 1925, 1926).

John A. Wilson, *The Burden of Egypt* (The University of Chicago Press, 1951).

D. J. Wiseman, *Chronicles of Chaldaean Kings* (London: Trustees of the British Museum, 1956).

G. E. Wright, *Biblical Archaeology* (London: Gerald Duckworth & Co., Ltd., 1957).

C. L. Woolley, *Excavations in Ur* (London: E. Benn, 1954).

GENERAL INDEX

Aqiwasha (= Achean), 97
Arabia, 28, 138, 139, 163
Arabs, 158, 169
Arabic, 13, 14, 21
Aram, 152
Aramaic, 150, 154, 155
Aram Naharaim, 12
Arbella, Battle of, 149
Ariaramnes, 142, 144
Arik-den-ilu, 114, 152
Arinna, 48
Armenia, 15, 43, 114
Arpad, 122, 125, 152
Arses, 149
Arsites, 147
Artaphernes, 146
Artatama, 113
Artaxerxes I, 108, 146f., 175
Artaxerxes II, 108, 148
Artaxerxes III, 109, 148-149
Arvad, 119, 131
Aryan, 15, 43, 77
Asa, 168
Ashdod, 99
Ashkelon, 99
Ashur, 24, 32, 34, 42, 110, 111, 115, 116, 118, 128, 130, 140, 150
Ashurbanipal, 39, 105, 106, 110, 113, 117, 130f., 134, 142, 172
Ashur-dan II, 117
Ashur-dan III, 122
Ashurdugul, 112
Ashur-etil-ilani, 132
Ashur-nadin-ahhe, 113
Ashur-nadin-apal, 121
Ashur-nadin-apli, 115
Ashur-nasir-pal I, 116
Ashur-nasir-pal II, 118, 119
Ashur-uballit I, 113, 115
Ashur-uballit II, 106, 133
Asia Minor, 27, 30, 44, 98, 111, 115, 140, 142, 148, 149
Asklepios, 58
Assyria, 19, 30, 33, 42, 84, 105, 106, 110, 111, 113, 118, 140, 143, 146, 167, 170, 172, 174
Assyrians, 32, 102
Astyages, 138, 140, 142
Aswan Dam, 74, 95, 96

Aten, 89, 90, 91, 93
Athaliah, 168, 169
Athens, 146
Athenians, 108, 146
Atum, 63, 64
Avaris, 77-79, 94, 96, 159
Avesta, 151
Axum, 103
Azariah (= Uzziah), 169, 170
Azriayau, 153

Baal, 22, 166
Baasha, 168
Baba-ahi-iddina, 121
Babylon, 15, 33, 37, 40-42, 45, 84, 88, 107, 110, 113, 115, 118, 121, 122, 125, 128, 132, 134, 135, 139, 143, 144, 146, 172-174
Babylonia, 142, 143, 146, 154
Babylonian Chronicle, 106, 130, 142
Babylonians, 106
Bactria, 147
Badari, 52
Bagdad, 23, 42, 77
Bagoas, 149
Bar-Rekub, 153
Bahrein, Island of, 30
Barhadad (= Benhadad), 119, 120, 153, 168
Bashan, 167
Bastet, Goddess, 101
Bathsheba, 163
Behistun Inscription, 21, 144, 150
Beirut, 46, 95
Bel-ibni, 129
Belshazzar (= Bel-shar-usur), 139
Benaiah, 164
Beni Hasan, 74, 158
Benjamin, 162, 165
Bethel, 165, 169
Bethshan, 94
Bigwai, 147
Bit Adini, 119, 123, 152, 153
Bit Agushi, 152
Bit Amukkani, 131
Bit Bakhyani, 152
Bit Halupe, 119
Bit Yakini, 121, 123, 125, 152

Mareshah, 168
Mari, 12, 24, 33, 34, 111, 112
Marianni, 43, 77
Martet-ites, 53
Maspero, G., 79
Massagetae, 143
Mastaba, 59, 62, 64
Matilu, 122
Mattiwaza, 46, 113
Medes, 15, 106, 132-134, 140f.
Media, 121, 122, 128, 133, 134,
    137, 138, 140f., 147
Medinet Habu, 87, 98, 99
Medum, 58
Megabyzus, 146, 147
Megiddo, 83, 107, 172
Mektire, 72
Memnon, Colossi of, 87
Memphis, 51, 56, 58, 61, 62, 64,
    66, 70, 73, 89, 104-106, 108,
    131, 144
Mendes, 108
Menes, 53, 55, 56
Mentor, 149
Mentuhotep, 70-72
Merenptah (= Merneptah), 79
    97, 98, 159
Merenre, 61
Merikare, 66, 70
Merimde, 52
Meritaten, 90
Meshannipadda, 24
Meshwesh, 97
Mesilim, 23
Mesopotamia, 11, 12, 19, 22, 25,
    29, 30, 34, 41, 43, 74, 76, 153
Meyer, Eduard, 53, 57, 85
Micah, 169
Middle Assyrian Kingdom, 113f.
Middle Bronze, 158
Middle Kingdom (Egypt), 70f.
Middle Minoan, 74
Midianites, 158
Midrash, 155
Mita, 125
Miltiades, 146
Mitanni, 42, 43, 46, 47, 83, 84,
    86, 88, 113, 114
Moabites, 158, 163, 168

Moeris, 103
Monotheism, 90
Montet, Pierre, 77, 96, 102
Montu, 70, 73
Mosaic Decalogue, 36
Moses, 156, 159, 160
Mosul, 18
Mummu, 38
Mursilis I, 40, 41
Mursilis II, 46
Mushki, 115, 125
Muwatallis, 46, 47, 95
Mykerinos, 59-61

Nabatean, 155
Nabateans, 12
Nabonidus, 29, 30, 107, 137f., 140
Nabopolassar, 132f., 140, 154
Nabu-shum-ishkun, 118
Nahum, 105
Nairi, 116, 117
Nanna, 29, 30
Napata, 84, 102-105, 108
Naplanum, 33
Naramsin, 28, 42, 135, 152
Narmer, 52, 55, 56
Nathan, 164
Naucratis, 107
Nebo, 122, 134
Nebti-name, 55, 56
Nebuchadnezzar I, 115
Nebuchadnezzar II, 107, 134f., 142,
    172-174
Nechab, 55
Nechen, 55
Neco I, 106, 107, 131
Neco II, 106-108, 134, 172, 173
Nectanebos I, 108, 148
Nectanebos II, 109, 148
Neferirkare, 61
Nefretete, 90
Negade, 22, 52, 55, 57
Nehemiah, 147, 150, 175
Neo-Babylonian Empire, 12, 134f.,
    154
Neolithic Culture, 18, 52
Nephthys, 64
Nergal, 138

Turukku, 112, 114
Tushratta, 46, 113
Tutenkhaten (= Tutenkhamun), 91-93
Tuthalia, 115
Twelfth Dynasty (Egypt), 72f.
Twentieth Dynasty, 98f.
Twenty-first Dynasty, 100f.
Twenty-second Dynasty, 100f.
Twenty-fifth Dynasty, 102, 128
Twenty-sixth Dynasty, 105
Tyre, 105, 107, 119, 121, 122, 130, 131, 137, 164

Ugarit, 22
Ukizer, 123
Ulamburiash, 40, 42
Ululai, 123
Umma, 25
Ummanmanda, 140
Unas, 61
Ur, 23, 24, 27, 29-31, 33, 57, 138, 158
Ur-III Period, 29f., 75, 110
Urartu, 114, 120, 122, 125, 128
Urhi-Teshup, 47
Urmia, Lake, 121
Urnammu, 29, 30, 36, 138
Urnansha, 25
Urshanabi, 40
Uruk, 20-25, 27, 29, 34, 39
Urukagina, 25
Ur-Zababa, 27
User-kaf, 61
Ushpia, 110
Utnapishtim, 39, 40
Utuhegal, 29
Uzziah (= Azariah), 122, 169, 170

Valley of the Kings, 81, 86, 92, 93, 95

Valley of the Queens, 99
Van, Lake, 43, 116, 122
Vartatua, 130
Vulture Stela, 25

Wadi Hammamat, 74
Warad-sin, 34
Warka, 19, 20
Wen-Amun, 100
Winckler, Hugo, 44, 48
Winlock, H. E., 66, 70
Wiseman, D. J., 135
Woolley, Leonard, 23, 57
Wosret, 73
Writing, 21

Xenophon, 148
Xerxes I, 108, 146
Xerxes II, 147
Xois, 76

Yahweh, 159, 160, 165, 166, 168, 172
Yamutbal, 33, 34
Yasmah-Adad, 34
Yaya, 73

Zadok, 164
Zagros Mountains, 29, 114
Zakre, 97, 99
Zakir, 153
Zechariah, 175
Zedekiah, 107, 137, 173, 174
Zerah, 168
Zerubbabel, 175
Ziggurat, 21, 22, 30, 34
Zimrilin, 34, 35
Zoan (= Tanis), 96
Zoroaster, 151
Zoroastrianism, 144